What Happened Yesterday

Matthew Sturniolo

ISBN: 978-1-956464-61-0

First Edition 2026

Published by BrightRay Publishing

To the younger version of myself—look at where we are now.

To you, the reader, taking time out of your life to hear about mine—I will forever be grateful.

Everything you want in life is yours.
Dream big, and let nothing hold you back.

Table of Contents

Yesterday

Sometime in 2003, my mom, eight weeks pregnant, walked into the hospital alone.

For a few days, she had some health complications and, concerned about her pregnancy, scheduled a very, very early ultrasound. Like any mom, the thought that something could be wrong with her baby caused her a lot of anxiety, but still, she insisted that my dad stay home with my older brother, Justin. Even when Dad objected and said, "No, I should go with you," she told him not to worry. Whatever news she got, she was strong enough to take it.

Or, at least, that's what she told herself. Actually sitting on the examination table while the sonographer quietly did the ultrasound . . . that was a different story.

"Is everything okay?" Mom asked, freaked out by the silence.

The sonographer didn't respond immediately. Instead, she just put more gel on her stomach and kept looking and looking. Mom had no idea what she was searching for or why she wasn't speaking, but whatever the reason, it was concerning.

"Did you do in vitro fertilization?" asked the sonographer.

"No?" replied my mom.

"Will you excuse me for a moment?"

The sonographer walked out of the room, leaving my mom lying there without a clue. When she returned, she had someone else next to her. That person then began doing the ultrasound, mumbling, "Yeah . . . Mhm . . . Are you sure you didn't do in vitro?"

My mom was getting impatient, frustrated that no one was telling her the problem. Suddenly, the two sonographers looked at each other and nodded.

"What's going on?" my mom finally asked.

No answer.

"What, am I having twins?" Mom joked.

"No," said the sonographer. "You're having triplets."

Even though there was no one else in the room, Mom looked around, trying to see who the woman was speaking to. In her mind, there was no way the sonographer was referring to her. Triplets? That happened in other families, not hers.

"Are you telling me I'm going to have three babies?" Mom asked, still in denial.

"Yes."

"Does that mean," she continued, "I'm *really* going to have three babies?"

The sonographer laughed. "You're going to have three beautiful babies!"

At that moment, several staff members burst into the room with gifts and cards. One handed my mom a teddy bear from the gift shop, holding a bouquet of three roses. Except, the roses were pink.

"Why are these *pink*?!" Mom panicked. "Am I having three girls?"

"No, no," the staff member apologized. "That was all they had in the gift shop."

My mom sighed in relief. She and my dad, first and foremost, wanted a healthy baby, but they were also secretly hoping for another boy.

Staring at the bear, a mixture of both anxiety and joy finally overwhelmed her.

Not *one* baby. *Three.*

Walking out of the hospital, she desperately wanted anyone to walk by so she could grab them by the shoulders and announce, "I'm having triplets!" She had to tell someone. Anyone. But instead, she held it together . . . well, until she made it to the parking garage.

Remembering where she'd parked, she went to press the button on the elevator. Suddenly, with her finger hovering over the number, it hit her.

She was parked on the third floor.

Three.

Of course, she thought, wiping tears from her eyes. Silently praying, she walked to her car, climbed in, and called my dad to tell him she was on the way home.

Later, when she first showed him the images from the ultrasound, Dad didn't get it.

"Why does it say one, two, and three on it?" he asked, putting the image closer to his face.

Mom smiled. "One baby," she said, pointing to each number. "Two babies, three babies."

My dad's mouth fell open. "You're kidding."

"No, I'm not."

The two of them sat there, just staring at the picture. They couldn't believe how big their family was about to grow. The idea of having three infants at one time definitely scared them, but they were also ready to take on the challenge. They'd figure it out. And they'd be great parents to all three of us.

Then, they realized: They still had to tell Justin.

His reaction went as expected—he hit the jackpot. He'd been begging and wishing for a younger brother forever. Well, turns out he wished too hard. Instead of one, he'd get three.

A few months later, me, Nick, and Chris were born.

And no, it's not *Nick, Chris, and I.*

It's *me, Nick, and Chris*.

I know it's grammatically incorrect—but that's the way it's been for our entire lives.

Raising *me, Nick, and Chris* was, predictably, not easy. Especially during that first year. In almost every one of our baby photos, there's my mom, dad, and at least one other person (whether that was my godmother, a family friend, or a relative) also in the picture. One baby for each person to hold.

When we got sick of being held and rocked to sleep, my parents would spend an eternity packing up our things and putting us in each of our car seats so we could drive around the neighborhood in the minivan. While most days may have been excruciatingly long, and my mom may have thought that she'd never have any free time, ever again—watching from the front seats as we slowly fell asleep, one by one, my parents felt just as much happiness as they did exhaustion.

Unlike a lot of twins, triplets, and quadruplets, we know that our parents never mixed us up as babies. I'm certain that baby Matt is adult Matt, and same for Nick and Chris. Not only did my parents paint our big toes different colors (mine blue, Nick's red, and Chris's orange), but Chris is the only one of us with a birthmark on his back. Also, for a while, Nick had to wear a helmet to make sure his head stayed round. Although, eventually, he had to stop wearing it because, like a bull, he'd swing his helmeted head into me and Chris, knocking us out cold in the crib we shared. Now, because he didn't wear his helmet for as long as he was supposed to, Nick's neck is permanently a little bent, but me and Chris being conscious was kind of more important.

My dad being at work, Mom had to take us everywhere with her, which meant loading up the van with changes of clothes, snacks, and a giant, three-seated stroller. No matter where she went—the grocery store, the park, the bank—she'd get stopped by someone every minute or so asking to see the babies and saying something like, "God *bless* you." Of course, she'd then have to recite the story of finding out, crying in the parking garage, and telling Justin. Everything is a big deal when walking around with triplets in public.

I cannot imagine how much more difficult this got when we all became toddlers. Having one toddler in a grocery store is hard enough. Three must have been a nightmare, with me, Nick, and Chris yanking toys and sugary cereals off the shelves, begging her to buy them, and running up and down the aisles. Before triplets, Mom finished her shopping in 20 minutes. But now, having to find three times the amount of food while wrangling us in and answering every stranger's questions, it took forever.

Thankfully, this whole ordeal became much, much easier as we aged. Some things, however, never change.

For instance, I've basically lived with three names my whole life. Anytime someone says "Matt," "Nick," or "Chris," all three of us look up. It doesn't matter if I think the person is talking to me or not. I still look, just in case they say "Nick" or "Chris" but really mean "Matt."

Even my mom, who can tell us apart (but might have to think about it for a second), calls us anything between "Matt," "Nick," "Chris," "Justin," or sometimes even "Trevor," our dog. There have been so many times when I've been standing right next to her in the kitchen while she's cooking, and she turns around and yells at the top of her lungs, "Matt! Food's ready!" Scenarios like this probably still happen a million times a day.

Something else that never changed: With us triplets, my older brother, my parents, and a dog all crammed in a two-story house, being "alone" was never an option. Even when you showered, there was a good chance someone would burst in to use the bathroom or brush their teeth.

Our childhood home was in Somerville, Massachusetts, the kind of place where you almost know everyone. Even though we weren't far away, we didn't have the pressures of a bigger city like Boston. Our school and a lot of stores were walkable from our house. Me, Nick, and Chris could walk to the sandwich shop, and the person behind the counter would be my mom's friend's husband or some distant relation like that.

It makes sense that we lived in a close-knit community since we were such a close-knit family. Everything I did, I did with my parents or my brothers nearby. When I was a kid, I never even thought about needing personal space. The only thing that really mattered was going to the park or riding our bikes after dinner.

Nick and Chris will be the first to say that, for a long time, we basically didn't have our own identities. Not because we or anybody else forced us to like the same things, but because, as kids, we didn't know what an identity *was*. We just knew we had each other. So, we had the same friends, wore the same clothes, and ran our opinions by each other to confirm we all thought the same way. We even shared the same bedroom for most of our lives.

At one point, Justin moved his bedroom from the end of the hallway to the second floor, and Chris called dibs on his old room. But even though Chris moved all his stuff in there, he never slept in it. Instead, we kept doing what we had always done: We pushed our two bunk beds together to create one big bed for all three of us. Me and Chris took the edges, and Nick slept in the middle, lying flat against the wood of the two bed frames with blankets and pillows shoved in there as cushions. It was like being packed in a sardine can. Sometimes, my dad would even come in and take a bunk for himself.

We went everywhere and did everything together. To leave out a triplet was unthinkable. It just didn't happen.

Actually, some of my first (and best) memories are from road trips, with me, Nick, Chris, and Justin shoved in the back of our mom's minivan, wreaking havoc while my mom and dad told us to quiet down from the front seats. Justin would stretch out over all the triplets, smothering us while we yelled back and forth at each other in some argument or another, on full rampages. For two or three hours—however long it took us to get from point A to point B—we wanted to tear each other's heads off, only for the actual vacation to be super fun and some of the best moments of our lives, even now.

Every summer, we drove to Cape Cod to stay in a coastal house my grandfather bought decades ago from a hunter. There's still a deer head on the wall to prove it. His name is Oscar, and he now wears my grandfather's old baseball hat.

Even though the Cape house had four bedrooms, only the adults slept in those. Not wanting to separate from each other and sleep in different places, the kids (my brothers, my cousins, my friends) would instead pile blankets and pillows on the living room floor. Plus, with our grandmother's old antique knickknacks everywhere—dolls, faded paintings, wind chimes, glasses, and plates that everyone refused to move out of respect for her—us kids really didn't want to be alone in that house. We'd start staring at the creepy dolls or Oscar the taxidermied deer head and freak ourselves out so much, we wouldn't be able to sleep. Instead, we lumped together on the floor, talking and laughing much later into the night than we should have.

As a kid, waking up early in the morning when you know you get to spend all day with your family and friends—and not at school—is the best feeling ever. The backyard of the house was literally just sand and water, but because it was not constantly flowing water, the sand felt more like slushy mud than a beach. This meant that, rather than make sand castles or swim in the ocean, we took out canoes and kayaks. With all the land surrounding the house, we also played a lot of cornhole, man hunt, and capture the flag. I remember, one time, I dropped my hat behind the couch, and when my dad reached behind to grab it, his elbow went straight through the thin wall. Since we did a lot of arts and crafts up there too, one of my brothers painted "Summer Fun in the Summer Sun" on a canvas, and my dad screwed it over the hole in the wall to hide it. That painting has been there for years, and there are still family members who don't know about it.

Moments like these defined my childhood. Really, they affected my teenage years, and they continue to impact what I want to do with my life going forward.

The woods were one of—if not the only—places where I felt truly at peace. Sitting under a tree, staring at the water with my family nearby, I was alone without being alone. Away from the city with all its people and traffic and dangers, I could just *be*.

I wasn't just a triplet. A kid with anxiety. A burden.

I was Matt.

Squirrels ran up trees around me. Ants climbed the log I sat on. Birds flew over the ocean. And all I had to worry about was catching the ice cream truck when I heard it coming up the road.

The following stories in this book are, in many ways, about the struggle to reclaim that peace in my everyday life. As me and my triplet brothers grew up, we somehow gained a fairly large following on the internet, especially on YouTube. So much of our lives is on display for millions of people around the world to see and comment on. For our viewers, it's no secret that I've struggled with anxiety for the majority of my life. What may be surprising, however, is how bad it really was.

That being said, I didn't write this as a "woe is me" story. I don't want pity from anyone. That's actually why I started the book this way—to show I had an amazing childhood and supportive family.

This is more of a thank-you note than a complaint letter.

Until now, I have never been vocal to anyone about how they helped me become who I am today. A lot of them will find out by reading this book. My therapist will read this and see that all of those endless hours of trying to figure out my emotions while we played Topple wasn't a waste of time. Ms. Summers will hear how she is the only reason I didn't let the troubles of middle school get the best of me. My dad will read that his hard work for our family of six was so gratefully appreciated and how, no matter what, I knew he was only a phone call away.

And my mom. Her words had the biggest impact on me. Because of her, I learned it's possible to leave your problems in the past to become a better and stronger version of yourself.

My mom was and is a very busy woman—the persistent, caring type who would work all hours of the day if it meant she could help even one more person. Chris always said that our mom could be the mayor of Somerville if she wanted because she knows so many people through her job.

My mom worked as a school helper at my brothers' and my elementary school while we were there. Then, after we left, she moved on to another school as a family liaison, where she continues to help lots of families in need, bringing food or staying with kids as they wait for parents to pick them up. Or she takes kids into the office who need help or even a moment away from the crowds. She calls herself an "unofficial social worker," tackling everything from housing needs for families to supporting teachers. My mom, who all the students knew as "Miss MaryLou," has helped everyone, but especially me. If I was going through a tough time as a kid, I would turn to her.

"Take everything one day at a time," my mom repeated. "Tomorrow is a brand new day."

Kids are impressionable. They look to the people they love for guidance. And a lot of times, after a hard day, I would sit on the edge of my bed and think about all the ways I wish things had gone differently.

Sometimes, my mom's words, "Get some rest. Tomorrow will be different," changed everything.

Does Everybody Have Anxiety?

I had my first anxiety attack at 10 years old.

March 2014. My Little League teammates, my triplet brother Chris (who was also on the team), my dad (the coach), and I had all sat down at a restaurant after our first game of the day. We had just spent the last half hour smiling in front of a camera for the team's picture day, and since we were playing a doubleheader and had another game that night, we walked to a restaurant two minutes away from the field for dinner, not seeing the sense in packing up and going home only to return to the backfield in an hour and a half for the second game.

The small restaurant could barely fit our baseball team. It had the vibes of a local diner, serving up greasy foods like tater tots, mozzarella sticks, and french fries from behind a counter. It was there that, sitting at pushed-together wooden tables, I felt, for the first time, a pit in my stomach.

My nerves bunched up, and sweat dripped down my face. That, combined with the sudden nausea, made everything feel urgent. For the few short years I'd been alive, my life revolved around sports, playing soccer, baseball, and hockey, but I had never felt anything like this before. My instincts screamed at me to run, somewhere, anywhere, away from other people. And I had to go *now*.

I bolted out of my seat and, hyperventilating, approached the register at the front of the restaurant. Before I could even ask an employee about the bathroom situation, I saw a laminated paper taped to the wall: "No public restrooms. Sorry."

Four words took away my chance at hiding. Bending over to clutch my stomach, I asked the woman behind the counter if there was a bathroom I could use. The lady, busy jotting down a long list of the team's orders, took one second to reach over, tap the laminated sign, and say, "Nope. Sorry, honey." Another devastating "*Sorry*."

I ran back over to the table. "Dad, I really need to go to the bathroom."

"Go run back to the concession stand at the field, and ask them for the key so you can use the bathroom there." That was the best he could do. He didn't know what I was going through, and he had to take care of all the other 10-year-olds on the team. I tried to stutter out another sentence, attempting to ask him to come with me, but I didn't even get the words out.

"You okay, buddy?" he asked.

"Mhm," I mumbled as I ran out of the restaurant to go back to the field.

If it's a two-minute walk and there's nobody in line at the stand, then I can quickly ask for the key in five seconds. If the key doesn't jam or if the door handle isn't hard to twist, then that's about a minute and 10 seconds, making a total of 3 minutes and 15 seconds until I'm hidden away from everybody.

Halfway through my sprint, more thoughts started to sink in.

It's so embarrassing you ran out.

Is the bathroom really going to help me?

Dad doesn't even know what's happening.

All I wanted to do was disappear. I made the decision to turn around and head back to the restaurant. Then, I started to overthink again.

I can't go back in there.

I don't know what's happening to me.

If I go back in there, it will be worse.

You're embarrassing yourself.

Outside, I found a corner of the building, where I stood by a four-foot-tall wire fence for five minutes—what will forever be the longest five minutes of my life. Five minutes that I returned to, again and again, for years after this.

My warm face became cold, drained of all color. Every negative thought I could think went through my head: *I am going crazy, I'm sick, I'm probably dying.* Any energy left in my body was used up from trying to figure out why I was so scared and upset. Everything was going great, but then all of a sudden, it was horrible. Finally, one of my teammates came outside. I'm grateful for him, but he was the last person I wanted to see. Everything was a joke or a game to this kid.

Choking down air with tears in my eyes and holding onto the wire fence, I looked over to him and asked, "Can you go back in there, get my dad, and tell him to come out here?"

"Sure, but I'm going to go and pee first." He started to walk toward the field.

"WAIT!" I yelled. "Can you go and get my dad first?" I tried to sound as desperate as I could. *Here it comes*, I thought. *Here come the stupid little jokes.*

"Why? Do you not want me to go into the bathroom because you peed on the floor?"

Stupid. Joke.

"Please, just go get my dad," I said.

"Alright, alright." He turned around to go back into the restaurant, and I stood there again, waiting. A part of me felt better knowing that my dad would help me soon, but every second it took for him to come outside felt longer and longer.

Turning the corner, Dad looked confused. He walked around the fence, grabbed me, and asked if I was okay. I didn't answer, instead saying over and over again with a shaky voice, "Please take me home. Please take me home."

"Okay, okay. Hold on, you're okay," he said. He pulled out his phone to call my mom, which is when I remembered she had dropped us off at the field. My dad didn't have his truck.

All odds were against me. There was nothing I could do to get home.

"Let's go inside and wait for Mom," he suggested.

"No!" I begged. He gave up on moving me anywhere, seeing that I was embarrassed. For 15 more extremely long minutes, my dad held me and rubbed my back, repeating that I would be fine.

I heard him. I just didn't believe him.

My mom eventually pulled up in front of the restaurant. I have never thrown myself into a car faster.

"What happened? Are you okay?"

I didn't answer, instead crawling to the other side of the car and holding my stomach. My dad, leaving the rest of the kids with the other coaches, followed me into the backseat, since my mom had a family friend in the passenger seat. They had a meeting at the elementary school where they both volunteered.

My mom and dad started talking about me, using words like "panic," "sick," and "random," but I drowned out what they said, instead looking out the window and counting the number of turns left until we got home. I wanted to butt in and tell them I would be fine; I just needed to go home. But I didn't say anything, knowing my mom's friend was in the car. I didn't want to explain to the friend why I interrupted their drive.

My mom pulled into our driveway and dropped us off. In the house, I immediately changed out of my baseball uniform and went to the bathroom. I got onto my knees in front of the toilet and tried to throw up. My dad followed me in soon after and rubbed my back while I tried to puke. I couldn't throw up anything.

Why can't I throw up? That's the feeling I'd had in my stomach for the last 45 minutes. Nothing. *What is going on?* I left the bathroom, sat on the couch with my dad, and took deep breaths.

As I sat there, the pain in my stomach slowly faded. I started to watch TV and didn't think about it. The next thing I knew, the pit was gone. The stomach pain that was killing me went away, not by throwing up but by simply sitting on the couch in my house. I was confused, but all I could think of was how I hoped, whatever this mystery stomach pain was, it never happened again. The five minutes I spent holding onto the metal wire fence outside of that restaurant felt like nothing else existed except that panic.

My dad shut off the TV. "How are you feeling? Better?"

I nodded. "Much better. I don't know what happened."

"Okay, good. Go put your uniform back on. We have to be there in 15."

My heart sank. I completely forgot I had another game to play.

"Let's get going, Matty." I put my baseball pants back on, and we went out to the truck. This time, he was driving just in case he had to bring me home again.

We drove back to the field, and my dad pulled in front of the concession stand and gave me 10 dollars. "Get me sunflower seeds, and get yourself a water and any candy you want."

"Okay, got it."

Before I closed the door, Dad said, "I'll park at the backfield. Meet me down there."

I had been going to this baseball park since I was born, watching my older half-brother Justin (who I never call my half-brother because, to me, he is just as much my brother as Nick and Chris) play, so I knew exactly where to go. Growing up, Justin was the blueprint for me, Nick, and Chris. A whole six years older, he was cool and confident, and nothing was a big deal. Being in high school, he didn't *ask* our mom if he could hang out with friends; he *told* her where he was going, and then he wouldn't come back home until *8:30 at night*. He played Guitar Hero and online poker, and he could do complicated math problems with parentheses and letters in them, something I couldn't even fathom since I could barely handle multiplication tables. Looking back, I can't believe he had to figure out life all by himself without a big brother to look up to. I knew, even then, that I would never be able to do what Justin did. Proof of this was that, here I was, thinking I was dying in the same ballpark where Justin used to play.

"I'll be right back," I said.

There were two people in front of me at the stand.

I clicked my cleats on the ground, folded the money, and unfolded the money again.

I watched my dad drive his truck toward the back.

Then, the second his truck left my sight, it happened again.

I put the money in my pocket, hopped out of line, and ran down an alleyway to the backfield while holding my stomach. The second I turned the corner to the back parking lot, I saw my dad walking toward the field to meet up with my team and the other coach.

Before anyone from my team could even look at me, I ran from the alley straight at him, gripped his arm, and said, “Dad, it’s happening again. I need you to take me home now.”

“Again, Matty? What’s up?” I didn’t answer. Even if I wanted to answer, I couldn’t. Just as confused as he was, I had nothing to say. He put me in his truck and started to drive home.

“I’m sorry, Dad. I can’t do it,” I said.

“Can’t do what?” he asked, worried.

“I don’t know. I-I-I don’t even know.”

He drove home, rubbing my back with one hand and driving with his other as I put my head into my palms and cried. “I don’t know what’s wrong with me. I don’t know what’s going on.”

“It’s okay, Matt. We’re going home.” After we pulled into the driveway and I changed out of my baseball uniform again, I sat on the couch, trying to calm down while I waited for my mom to come home. My stomach didn’t hurt anymore, but I still laid down, playing mind games with myself and trying to figure out why I acted the way I did.

What did I eat today?

How much did I sleep last night?

Did I get hit by a ball or something?

When my mom walked through the door, she went right to me. My dad had already filled her in on the phone.

“Hi, Matt. How are you doing?” my mom asked me the second she reached the top of the steps leading into the house.

“I couldn’t do it,” I said.

“Couldn’t do what?”

“I don’t know. I just needed to go home. I don’t know what happened to me.” I moved to the edge of my seat, feet on the floor, and looked at her.

"Okay, you had a panic attack. It's normal," she said. "You got overwhelmed because you had a lot to do today."

"Why did my stomach hurt so bad?" I was 10 years old. I didn't understand how something mental could cause legitimate pain.

"You were anxious," she explained. "When you're anxious, it can cause your body to feel things physically as well." I blinked at her again, not getting it.

"It's okay, Matt. You're going to be fine. What you were feeling is normal, and there's nothing wrong with you," my mom repeated.

"Does everybody have anxiety?" I asked her.

"Yes, anxiety attacks happen to everyone. I've had anxiety attacks, and so has Dad."

I didn't understand how *everyone* could have anxiety. Why is it that I could live every day without a *care* in the world, but then one day, sitting in a restaurant or waiting in line for water and a pack of sunflower seeds, it can feel like the *end* of the world?

"You'll be okay. I promise. You just had a moment."

"Okay," I replied softly.

After that conversation, I lay down on the couch for a bit and then went to bed for the night. I wanted the day to be over so that I could wake up the next morning and forget all about what happened yesterday. I didn't even want to think about having an anxiety attack again in my life.

For the next month, I felt like a piece of myself was still standing there in that corner between the fence and that restaurant. Anytime something remotely wasn't going my way, I would think back to that moment, about what happened to me, and it would only make things harder.

I never thought, *Well, it could be worse. I could be having a panic attack like I did that day!*

Instead, I thought, *It's going to happen to me again soon. I just don't know when.*

COFFEE

What Do I Call Him?

On April 6, 2014, I woke up at 3 a.m. to go to the bathroom. As I walked down the hallway, I noticed the light was on in my parents' room, and the door was open. Looking in, I saw that they weren't there, and the way their blankets were crumpled up looked like they left in a rush. I went to the phone and called my mom's number, but my dad picked up. I asked him where he was, and he told me that he and my mom went to help Grandpa. It was normal for my mom and dad to visit him, but at 3 a.m., with all the lights turned on in their room and downstairs, I knew in my heart that something bad had happened.

I asked my dad, "Is everything okay? Will you be home soon?"

"Yeah, buddy, everything's okay. Sorry we scared ya. You can go back to bed."

"I will." I paused, not wanting to hang up the phone. "I love you."

"I love you too. Be home soon." I went to my room and tried to fall asleep, but too many thoughts swarmed in my head.

My grandpa, my mom's dad, started losing his battle with lung cancer around the same time I started having panic attacks. Always around during my childhood, he would often pop by our house to check on all of us but especially me and my brothers. Some of my fondest memories of him are extremely ordinary: He and my grandmother would spoil us by taking us to Target and Burger King. One day, he bought us two toys from Skylanders: Giants, a video game we liked.

My mom helps anyone and everyone, so when her dad was diagnosed with cancer, she stayed by his side almost every second of the day. As my struggles with mental health were just beginning, I stayed home with them while my brothers went out with friends. This meant I saw my mom and her dad build a relationship because of his cancer, which lasted for one year.

The night he died, I turned on my back, looked up at the ceiling, and just thought. I thought about all of the memories I had with my dad. I thought about how much time my mom had spent with hers over the past year. I thought about everyone: my brothers, my mom, my dad, my grandma, and my cousins. I thought about spending Christmas Eve together as a family. And then I thought about my grandpa.

I thought about how, every time he came over, I would go downstairs and open the door for him, and he would go up the stairs first, apologizing for being so slow that I had to wait behind him. I thought about how he would call my mom to make sure we were all doing okay. I thought about him sitting in the backyard and watching me and my brothers play catch with a football. He would sit and laugh.

And I thought about the journey he took as an immigrant from Portugal to come to Massachusetts to raise his kids. My grandparents raised my mom and her three brothers in Cambridge. When my grandpa first moved from Portugal to the United States at 23 years old, he didn't own any shoes. He worked hard by cleaning buildings and would bring my mom and all of her brothers to help clean windows for money. He taught my mom and my uncles the importance of hard work and how to build a business.

As soon as he saved up enough, my grandpa bought Dunkin' Donuts franchises. My uncles would work at one specific Dunkin' location near Saugus, where my dad grew up, so whenever we visited my dad's family, we would stop by, and my grandpa or uncles would walk us behind the counters where we could pick out whatever donuts we wanted. I'd make myself a vanilla bean Coolatta, which was basically a slushie but with flavored syrup and milk. The Dunkin' chains were eventually sold, but those memories remain with me.

I think those memories were important to my grandpa as well. He worked hard to keep his family close, even buying houses so that his children and grandchildren could live close to him. For the majority of my life, I lived in the same house as my aunt and uncle, who took the first floor while my family stayed on the second and third. Another uncle and his family lived in a house just up the road from ours, right next door to my grandparents and my third uncle, who lived on the bottom floor of my grandparents' house. In total, Grandpa owned three properties to ensure his family raised their kids next to him. In my eyes, everything he did was to make sure all of us were safe and happy.

Lying in bed and remembering this, I eventually fell asleep. The next morning, me, Nick, and Chris went into our parents' room and climbed onto the bed. My mom and dad were also awake.

Me and my brothers could tell that we interrupted the middle of a conversation. After lying there together for a while, my mom broke the news to us. "You guys know how Grandpa has been getting worse lately?" We nodded our heads. "Me and Dad went to see him last night because they called us and told us he wasn't doing very well. We stayed there for the night, and he passed in his sleep." We all had a feeling he was gone. Like me, Chris had gotten up in the middle of the night to use the bathroom and, seeing my parents' empty bedroom, had the same thoughts I did. When he reentered our room and climbed into bed, Nick woke up and instantly felt that me and Chris were upset. Knowing that Grandpa had not been feeling well that past week, he connected the dots. We had all arrived at the same conclusion—that something bad had happened to Grandpa—without saying a word to each other. Now, hearing that our fears had come true, we were devastated. But being kids without the words to describe our feelings, we stared at the ceiling in silence.

"I was there when he fell asleep. He showed no sign of pain or struggle," my mom added. "He's up in heaven now." Only 10 years old, I didn't know how to react. It was the first time in my life I had lost someone close to me. I'm not even sure when we crawled out of bed and got dressed. I only remember having the conversation and then all of us lying around for hours.

A few days went by before I went back to school. Everything felt strange to me. I was in class, sitting at my desk as my teacher gave a lesson, but nothing felt real. I clicked all of the lead out of my mechanical pencil, then pushed the lead back in over and over again. That's all I could focus on.

Turns out, the teacher was giving important instructions about the fifth-grade science fair. As I zoned back in, I heard her say, "Okay, turn to the person at the desk next to you, and give them three ideas for what you want to do your project on."

The boy who sat next to me was a nice kid. Being my brother's friend, he made sure I understood things and cracked jokes with me a lot.

He turned to me and asked, "Do you want to share first, or should I?"

"Can you go first? I'm not really sure yet," I replied.

"Yeah, I got you." He then said something about plants and light and the Sun, but even though I heard every word, I still didn't understand. Not because I didn't get his idea, but because I was drowning out everything.

"That sounds great," I said to him.

"Okay, cool. You go now before I give my other one."

For some reason, I felt like I had to tell him.

"Um, you know how I told you my grandpa had cancer?"

"Yeah?"

"He died a few days ago."

"Oh, man. I'm so sorry, Matt. That's terrible." Not knowing what else to say and sensing I didn't have anything else to add, he slowly turned away and looked back at the front of the room.

I had no idea why I said that to him. We were not best friends by any means—not even friends really. I didn't hang out with him often, only during the class we shared and occasionally at a mutual friend's house. Part of me just felt like I had to get it off my chest.

A couple of days passed. I woke up early for my grandpa's wake. My mom and dad had gone to wakes and funerals before, but this was a first for me. I didn't know how they worked. In the chaos of grief and funeral arrangements, no one had explained death to me in the way that you explain it to kids: that Grandpa's body remained on Earth, but his spirit was in heaven. Standing in front of an open casket, I didn't realize that was the last time I'd ever see him.

Me and my brothers had written him a card, and I had drawn him a picture of the two of us together. My mom opened his suit jacket, took the cards and my drawing, and put them inside his pocket. I walked out of the room with Nick and Chris, but from the doorway, I could see the rest of my family saying their final goodbyes.

As soon as she saw her sons had left the room, my mom let out a loud sob. She had been trying to be strong for us, but the moment we left her sight, the dam inside her broke. She screamed over and over, "Daddy, Daddy! No!"

My uncle hugged her: "It's okay. He's in heaven. He's home." He rubbed her back, and she cried into his shoulder, which didn't do much to muffle the sound. I had never seen my mother like that, and I haven't seen her that way since.

My mother and grandpa were not close for many years. It was after his lung cancer diagnosis that they started to understand one another. For the year before his death, he and my mom were always together. Whatever conflicts they had in the past were no longer as important as their relationship.

After my uncle reassured my mom, me and my brothers walked back into the room. She was doing better, still very sad but keeping it together. We stood there while family and friends said their goodbyes and that they were sorry for our loss. I didn't know what to do when people I hadn't seen in years, and people who I didn't even remember (because the last time they saw me, I was a baby), told me they were sorry for my loss. Not able to find the words, I just nodded in response.

At the end of the night, me and my brothers went to get dinner while my mom and dad stayed there. My mind raced, and I thought over and over about what my mom was dealing with. Other than that, I don't remember anything after leaving.

We sat in the church the next day for the funeral, listening as the priest gave the service. I had another moment where I looked down at my shoes and zoned out of the world around me. Sometime during me sitting half-in and half-out of reality, my dad was called up to say a few words.

I watched him walk up, grab the cards he had written, and begin his speech. He started with a story about how he never knew what to call my grandpa when he first met him.

"Do I call him by his first name? Do I call him Mr. Correia? What do I call him?" My dad took a breath. Voice shaking and tears rolling down his face, he said, "I never knew what to call him until I had kids. Then, I got to call him 'Grandpa.'"

That was the first time I saw my dad cry. Remembering my mom at the wake the day before put everything into perspective for me, and sitting in church, I recognized how important my parents were to me. I obviously had loved and cared about my parents before, but at that moment, it dawned on me that, one day, they weren't going to be here.

And I couldn't handle that.

Am I Really That Far Behind?

Right before fifth grade ended, I was scheduled to see a neuropsychologist for an evaluation. A teacher had pulled my mom aside and told her I wasn't reading at my grade level. Teachers technically aren't supposed to have these conversations with parents, but my mom, shocked to hear I wasn't retaining information in class, thanked the teacher and asked the school to do a neuropsych test. During the test, I was told to look at numbers, colors, and shapes, which led to me being diagnosed with "not being able to sit still." They didn't call it ADHD, but the consensus was that I couldn't focus on the same task for long periods. I couldn't sit still, or I would shut down.

The results meant that I'd need extra help when I got into sixth grade, which was no surprise to me. My class kept moving on to new subjects just as soon as I was starting to learn the last one. Still, I may have *needed* an IEP (individual education plan), but I definitely wasn't proud of it. To me, the *I* in IEP may as well have stood for "idiot."

We were now old enough that kids started to take Spanish classes, but every time Spanish class came around, I was pulled out to have a one-on-one lesson about material from my other classes. I felt embarrassed whenever the Spanish teacher came in to teach all of my other classmates, and I would have to walk from my assigned seat on the other side of the room, past everyone, to go into another classroom with two teachers just for me. All so I could catch up to what everyone else understood the first time they were taught it.

One day, I went into the small side classroom and sat with my teacher.

"Okay, Matt, let's pick a book to read today." My teacher and I walked over to the small bookshelf in the corner of the room, and I noticed that the book I was reading in my English class was on the shelf labeled "sixth-grade reading level." Instead of picking that book, my teacher reached past the entire shelf, landing on the fourth-grade books, and grabbed three for me to pick from.

Am I really that far behind?

"You can pick," I told her, too ashamed to choose for myself.

"I'm reading this one with two other students," she said, putting one of the books on the table in front of us. "So we'll do this one because it's fresh on my mind."

I grabbed my copy and opened it to the first page. She had me read the first chapter out loud, and even though I didn't stutter once and didn't need any help with the words, I didn't feel proud of myself. You'd think failure would have upset me the most, but the really strange feelings bubbled up when I did well. *Well, obviously, you should be doing well*, I'd think. *You're reading a fourth-grade book while being in sixth grade.*

I would have never been that hard on someone else in my shoes, yet I kept finding ways to make my accomplishments seem like the bare minimum. But why shouldn't I? I was behind.

Every day for a while, I would go to school, do my regular classes, and at the end of the day while everyone else stayed in Spanish, I would go to what I called my "stupid kid classes." After we finished the fourth-grade book, we started another but, this time, an "advanced" fourth-grade book. The next month, I read a fifth-grade book, and the month after that, I read an advanced fifth-grade book. We continued like this until I entered my actual sixth-grade reading level, which I hit in the middle of the year, and we re-read the book that my classmates and I read in our English class at the beginning of the year. Because I had already read it for class and remembered a lot of the story, the whole re-read was pretty easy for me. But I wasn't happy with my learning. The teacher would ask me in-depth questions about the books, and I never knew how to answer them. Sometimes, I felt like she would purposely ask me hard questions just so she could remind me that I was still dumb and needed the extra help.

Hanging out after school, friends would ask, "Hey, Matt, did you do the Spanish homework?"

I would reply, "They won't let me take Spanish because I barely know English."

Laughing, they'd say something along the lines of, "My bad. I forgot you weren't in that class." I learned to make fun of myself so no one else had the opportunity to.

Halfway through the school year, I accepted that extra help was here to stay. I still hated it, but at a certain point, I became numb. Sometimes, stress and that "stupid" feeling would catch up to me and make me feel what I felt that day at baseball again: shortness of breath, like something was weighing down on me and I had to get out, go anywhere else, just *away*. Thankfully, that's when my mom worked at our elementary school as a helper, so I could go to her if I needed to. Whenever I felt panicked, I could leave class and find her in the halls or in an office. Every time, she'd say a million kind and encouraging words, but all that really mattered was her presence. With just the sight of her, I was okay.

I couldn't have gotten through a school day without my mom. When the year ended, my K–6 school threw a moving-on ceremony—a mini-graduation for those of us entering the seventh grade. Me and my brothers wanted to give our mom a special gift since she'd spent so much time helping everyone in the school, so we went around to our classmates and their parents, asking them to contribute an item to a large thank-you basket. We bought her a pair of flip-flops, candy, a blanket, and other goodies, which we wrapped in a big, purple basket. At graduation, after every kid had walked down and accepted their certificate, my teacher and my brother went up to the podium, gave a short thank-you speech, and presented my mom with the gift.

Everything my mom does for people, she does out of the kindness of her heart. She never expects anything in return. Holding the basket, she began crying, which only became more intense once the teacher told her it was her sons' idea. I've never been good at expressing my gratitude for someone, but after the ceremony, I gave my mom a big hug. She knew, ever since that day at baseball, I needed her around. She also knew it wasn't practical; I couldn't be by her side every day for the rest of my life. I recognized that too. I just didn't want to believe it.

When summer ended, I'd be in a new school with new teachers and new students. And without my mom.

Matthew O. Sturniolo
Birth Date: 8/1/2003

Chief Complaint

- Anxiety
- Attention-deficit hyperactivity disorder
- Academic problems

History of Present Illness

Matthew Sturniolo is a 12-year-old male. The source of patient information was his mother:

Matthew is a triplet who is suffering immensely from anxiety.

He started seventh grade at a new school. He did go in for the first couple of days but is now begging us not to leave him. We have asked him what he thinks is going on, and he expresses a fear of something bad happening if he goes to classes.

He has spent hours with the school counselor in her office and is missing most classes. His brothers, who go to the same school, are supporting him and trying to encourage him, but he will not go. Each morning is an intense scene with the staff at the school peeling him off of me or my husband.

Matt has experienced anxiety and fear in the past but never to this degree. You do not accept our insurance, but I will pay out of pocket.

We are desperate to help our son. Thank you!

Notes

Patient (Pt) is struggling with the transition to his new school. It is much larger than his elementary school, and he is no longer in classes with his other triplets. Pt does not have social anxiety; he is very outgoing and has many friends. He gets anxious about transitions and new situations. Has been having panic attacks every day with nausea, shortness of breath, and chest pain. Pt wants to get better and go to school. He has a very supportive family. Pt has an IEP for ADHD and reading LD. No other psych distress. Tx only.

Personal History

- Education: 7th grade
- IEP for ADHD
- Reading LD
- Lives with parents and three brothers

When Do You Feel Joy?

A new school meant starting over from scratch, with yet another IEP teacher who'd talk to me way too slowly: "*Hiii, Maaatt . . . Hooow are you doooing?*" Thankfully, I had two and a half months before I had to worry about school.

In those months, I started therapy. The idea of it kept popping up, but I was a stubborn kid and didn't like the idea of a stranger knowing anything about me. Especially the things I didn't like about myself. Whenever I felt anxious, I tried to hide it, not wanting people to think I was a problem or a burden. And while my mom never thought that, she saw through my act every time. It became clear to her that when summer break was up and school started again, I'd be a total mess without her.

To be honest, I had no hope for therapy. I mean, how would talking to a stranger, who's being paid to listen, help me feel better? Seemed like a scam to me. I only told my mom I'd give it a shot because if I told her the truth, that I thought nothing would work and that I was unfixably broken, she'd be crushed. So, I did go to my first therapy appointment with hope. Just not *my* hope.

Walking into the brick building, I felt like I was seeing a doctor or dentist. The front desk, numbered offices, and waiting room felt too clean. The room even had that Clorox smell.

After a few minutes, an upbeat, way-too-excited, middle-aged lady with a high ponytail and business casual blazer came out of the room. My therapist, Jessie. She seemed like the type to make everything a big deal.

"Hi, Matt. It's nice to meet you, buddy," she said. I didn't reply.

"Hi, Mom." She directed her attention to my mom and hugged her. "Come on in, come on in."

While Jessie and my mom talked, I looked around her office. It looked like my kindergarten classroom, with all kinds of posters, games, and toys. My mom filled her in on what my anxiety looked like: the day at baseball, my school life, and how I acted at home. Jessie then explained how she intended to help and her expertise, all while including me in the conversation by making eye contact with me and breaking down what she meant. Using games and pictures to understand emotions, she said, it wouldn't feel like therapy at all.

I don't think I spoke a single word the entire time, even though the whole point was for her to understand me more. On the walk back to the parking lot, my mom asked how I thought it went. All I said was, "Good."

"Well, what do you think of her?"

"She's nice," I said. "I really like the *Inside Out* posters on her wall." The movie had recently come out, so walking into her office, I was surprised she already had a poster.

My mom agreed: "We're going to try this out." The whole therapy thing wasn't supposed to be stressful. All it could do was help. I nodded, hopped in the car, and tried not to overthink on the way home.

I saw my therapist again a week later. This time, without my mom.

The point of therapy is to calm your nerves, talk about your emotions and feelings, and figure out why you feel them. But walking into that building, I was the most nervous I'd been in a while. Even though Jessie was a therapist, I thought she wouldn't hear me or that she'd discover my feelings made no sense at all. Being so young, I had no way of knowing what anxiety was. For all I knew, I had a terminal disease that could send me into cardiac arrest at any minute.

Sitting at a table in her office, Jessie asked me about my week.

"Good."

"What was your favorite thing you did?"

"Stayed home and watched TV." All I wanted to do that summer was lock myself in the house. My brothers would hang out with friends, but I wouldn't go. At home, nothing could go wrong. I couldn't bring myself to leave the safety or familiarity. The schedule I set for myself was dependable, predictable, and easy: sleep, watch TV, and when the stomach pains came, try to throw up.

"What did you do outside of the house last week?"

I didn't have anything to tell her.

"Why don't you go with your brothers when they go over to your friends' houses? Or run errands with your mom?"

"I don't feel good when I have to do those things," I replied.

"Okay, why do you think that's happening?"

The simple question pissed me off. If I knew *why* that was happening, I wouldn't need therapy. I would do something about the anxiety myself. Instead of saying that, I responded, "Not sure."

"We're going to do a little exercise so we can start to understand your emotions. That way, we can figure out what's causing them." Jessie asked if I'd ever seen *Inside Out*, and when I said yes, that I really liked it, she became excited, telling me the exercise had to do with the movie.

A second copy of the *Inside Out* poster appeared on the table in front of us. If you've never seen it, *Inside Out* is an animated movie about an 11-year-old girl named Riley who deals with intense emotions, depicted as five characters: Joy, Sadness, Anger, Fear, and Disgust. Jessie pointed at the Sadness character on the poster.

"When do you feel the most like her?"

"When I'm away from my mom or dad. When I can't see them."

She pointed at Anger and asked the same question.

"I feel angry when I'm away from my mom or dad," I said again.

She went on to ask me the same question about the characters Fear and Disgust, and I gave her an identical response each time.

Finally, she put her finger on Joy. "When do you feel the most like her?"

"When I get to stay home with my family."

Jessie raised her eyebrows and smiled. "That's very nice, Matthew. I'm going to ask you one more question, okay, buddy?"

"Okay . . ."

"When do you feel joy, apart from when you're with your family?"

She stumped me. I looked at the poster and opened my mouth, trying to give her an answer, but as I looked back at the last year, I realized every single happy memory included my mom or dad.

"I don't know," I said. For two seconds, she lost her smile. Then, she noticed I was staring at her, not the poster, and the grin returned, but this time a little forced.

"Okay. That's okay," Jessie said. "We'll find something."

We spent the rest of the session going over school, sports, and friends' houses, all while I pointed at different emotions on the poster. I explained to her that when I would play hockey, I wouldn't go on the ice unless I could see my mom on the bleachers first. Or, if my brothers went to my friend's house to swim in her pool, I wouldn't go unless all the moms were invited too. When she asked me about school, I explained that my mom worked at my school.

Soon after, my session was up.

I wouldn't see this until many years later, but my mom had copies of all the notes made by Jessie during our appointments. On the top of every report was the name, "Matthew O. Sturniolo." I don't know if this was because my mom had to juggle multiple kids' names or if Jessie wrote down the information incorrectly during our first appointment, but Matthew O. Sturniolo was not sitting in those therapy sessions—Matthew B. Sturniolo was. My middle name is Bernard, after my grandfather. In hindsight, it didn't affect the quality of care, but it's just another sign that I was not connecting with therapy.

My mom and Jessie saw my immediate diagnosis as progress, but I only felt like it validated that something was wrong with me: I had both separation anxiety and depression. My brothers, Nick and Chris, who I experienced every moment of the day with, weren't even remotely close to feeling what I felt. If they were fine, then I must've been wired wrong. And I knew my mom was concerned about how everyone felt, from the students she works with to family members. I knew she must have been worried about me and if I would get better.

Two weeks went by, and the diagnosis weighed on my mind.

Would I ever feel happy without my mom next to me?

38

Where's the Cheese?

Mom grabbed a pink ticket at the deli counter: number 38. The sign said they were serving number 35, so she had three people ahead of her in line.

Earlier that afternoon, she'd asked me and my brothers if we wanted to go grocery shopping. We all agreed, but I was the only one who left the car to go inside the store while my brothers wanted to stay and listen to music on the radio. I couldn't wait in the car without her, so instead, I walked with my mom in the store, grabbing the groceries she pointed at and throwing them into the cart when we stopped at the deli.

With only four more items on her shopping list, my mom turned to me and said, "I'm gonna go grab some produce." She motioned to the exact spot she'd be in and handed me the ticket. "You wait here. When they call number 38, ask for half a pound of American cheese, so Dad can grill cheeseburgers tonight." The pink deli slip felt like a brick in my hand.

"I'll be right over there when you're done," she said, then walked all the way to the other side of the store. This was my moment to be strong. I would prove to myself that I could function without my mom always by my side. As I watched her get farther and farther away, the service sign number ticked to 36. Two more people, two more orders, and I'd be good. No way it'd take longer than three minutes. Four minutes tops.

I looked at the sign. I looked at my mom across the store. I looked back at the sign. The man behind the counter smiled at a customer. Another man ordered some kind of sliced meat. I lost sight of my mom, scanned the store for her again, and found her, grabbing a vegetable and checking it off her list. When she started to walk toward me, I sighed in relief.

But then, she turned down an aisle. I lost sight of her.

Even though there were only a few people around me, I felt like they were all watching and judging me. What did they think of me? Did they know I was panicking? I wanted to go home.

Tears formed in my eyes. My feet pushed off the ground, and I ran to the aisle where I last saw my mom, pushing aside any cart or person in the way. When I finally found her, I grabbed onto the sides of the cart, panting.

"That was fast," she said. "Where's the cheese?"

I didn't know how to answer. I just reached into my pocket and held out the pink ticket, not picking my head up to look at her. She grabbed it out of my hand, and we walked over to the deli stand again, not saying a word.

She knew I had another panic attack. The second I found her, I felt fine, but for the rest of the trip, I kept thinking, *What's wrong with me? Why do I get like that?*

I couldn't understand it, which only made me more frustrated.

My therapist said she was proud of me, that my attempt in the grocery store was a "step in the right direction." We talked more about how, if I kept challenging myself, then eventually I would "be okay."

That was hard for me to hear. I didn't want to keep challenging myself because I knew how "great" it went the last time.

Matthew O. Sturniolo
Birth Date: 8/1/2003

Chief Complaint

- Anxiety
- Attention-deficit hyperactivity disorder
- Academic problems

History of Present Illness

Family describes that Pt wants to go to school the night before, but in the morning, the anxiety starts and increases as school approaches. Family shared that the anxiety started after an incident in 2014. Pt did not want to stay for a baseball game and went home. Parents report that Pt showed no anxiety before this incident. Since then, he wants to know where his parents are if they are out of the home.

Overall, his parents shared that Pt is a cautious child, immature for his age, and if there is any type of distress, he wants his parents around.

Target Symptom:

- Anxiety
- Frequency: Often
- Intensity: Severe
- Status: No change

Target Symptom: School Attendance

- Frequency: Often
- Intensity: Severe
- Status: No change

Therapy

Pt acknowledged he jumps to the worst-case scenarios in his mind. Discussed learning to change his thoughts.

Skills Taught/Reinforced

- Expressing thoughts/feelings
- Identifying dysfunctional thoughts/behaviors
- Identifying patterns

BACK TO
SCHOOL

Can I Go to the Bathroom?

On August 1, 2015, I turned 12. I couldn't believe that in a year's time, I'd be a teenager, not a little kid anymore.

As much as I looked forward to teenagehood, the arrival of August also meant something else: The beginning of a new school year. The first day of seventh grade. A break in routine. *Middle school.*

The first morning, groups formed on the basketball court almost immediately. The kids from my old school stood together, and the kids from the new school, who'd also gone there last year for elementary school, stood across from them. No one wanted to be the first to switch sides. Eventually, though, the two groups slowly merged into one, once they started recognizing each other from sports, church, or their parents being friends. A lot of my teammates from hockey went to the other school during sixth grade, so now, I'd get to see them during the day, not just at practice. I realized that, as much as people liked to pretend the switch from elementary to middle school didn't matter, the new territory marked an important milestone in our lives. This would be the first test: Which friends would stick, and which friends would drift away?

After talking on the basketball court, everyone—all 125 of us—had to navigate the hallways and find our homerooms by pushing, shoving, and weaving through crowds. No one knew the terrain—not even the kids who'd attended the same school since kindergarten. The middle school wing was a completely different section of the building. The only reason I didn't immediately freak out was because I had Nick with me. He told me he'd walk me to my homeroom before he went to his.

Elbowing our way through the sea of kids, I heard two girls say behind us, "There's no way these little shorties are in our grade." They laughed and walked past us. It was the craziest thing for me. I was short growing up, but no one had ever made fun of me for it. It blew my mind that during the first interaction with someone at this school, they mocked my height. The whole scene felt staged, like I was the lead role in a cheesy Disney original movie.

As one of the first three people in my homeroom, I didn't recognize any other students until my friend walked in. We talked about our summers, he showed me how the bands on his braces changed colors, and he introduced me to another kid next to him.

He gave me a nod and said, "Nice to meet you."

I said, "Hi."

Silence.

My friend cut in: "His name's Matt." The other boy laughed.

How stupid am I that I can't even introduce myself properly? I thought.

Before we could talk more, our teacher walked in front of the board and began detailing our insane schedules. Instead of two teachers, like we had in elementary school, we'd have four who all taught their own subjects, plus an "extra help" class. We went from two teachers to five traditional teachers, one "extra help" teacher, and a homeroom teacher—all in all, seven. I was overwhelmed.

Every class from there followed the same basic pattern. The teacher would tell us what to expect that year in terms of projects and workload, and then we'd all go around and answer the question: What's one unique thing about you?

My answer to every icebreaker was the same: "I'm a triplet."

The day was almost over. I knew because I had said the word "triplet" what felt like a thousand times, so much that it stopped sounding like a word at all. I only had one more icebreaker to sit through in math class, so I found my seat, ready for another hour of hearing what weird pets people owned and stories of cruise-ship vacations. But instead, my math teacher, who I'll call Mr. G, ran through his plans for the class like a military sergeant, strict and by the book. I couldn't tell if he was in a bad mood or simply the worst teacher ever.

"This is how the bathroom works in my class," Mr. G said. "There are four quarters in the school year. Each one of those quarters equals one bathroom pass. If you go to the bathroom four times in the first quarter, then you are out of bathroom passes for the year. I will expect you to hold it until class is over." The pit in my stomach grew.

The bathroom was one of my safe places. When I got stomach pains, all I wanted to do was be home, but the bathroom was the next best option, being the only place in public where I could have a break in isolation. Half the time I went to the bathroom in school, I wasn't using it; I just needed to check if I had to throw up, which I rarely did. As soon as Mr. G finished speaking, I raised my hand.

"Can I go to the bathroom?"

He let me go, but as I put my hand on the doorknob to leave, I heard him say to the class, "He has three more."

Matthew O. Sturniolo
Birth Date: 8/1/2003

Chief Complaint

- Anxiety
- Attention-deficit hyperactivity disorder
- Academic problems

History of Present Illness

Pt is going to school daily. He continues to have anxiety in the morning before school and needs his parents to take him.

Pt noted that changing his thoughts at school has been helpful. Mom noted that he is not getting his work done at school. Pt noted he is choosing not to do it and knows he needs to do it. He would like to see if he can get it done without taking medication.

Discussed how to change his thoughts in the morning before he goes to school to help decrease anxiety. Discussed how Mom can help support him in changing his anxious thoughts.

Target Symptom: Anxiety

- Frequency: Often
- Intensity: Moderate
- Status: Improved

Target Symptom: School Attendance

- Frequency: Never
- Intensity: Absent
- Status: Improved

Skills Taught/Reinforced

- Expressing thoughts/feelings
- Grounding techniques
- Identifying dysfunctional thoughts/behaviors
- Identifying patterns
- Rational self-talk
- Distraction methods
- Parenting strategies

SHO

Seven and a Half Hours?!

My biggest fear happened again one morning when my mom dropped me and my brothers off for school. Dragging my backpack out of the car and to the doors of the building, I turned around for a brief moment to watch my mom pull away.

And there it was. That pit in my stomach.

But, this time, worse.

In so much pain, I almost fell to the ground. I ran as fast as I could, right at her car. My mom didn't see me at first, but before she could put the car in drive, I launched myself at the window and started banging on it. *Bang, bang, bang*. I grabbed at the handle and pulled it over and over in a panic.

Confused, she pulled back into the parking spot and unlocked the car. I threw open the passenger-side door, jumped into the seat, and started screaming, crying, hyperventilating. I couldn't make out full sentences, not even to explain why it felt like I was falling apart from the inside out.

Yelling, punching the dashboard, hiding in my seat.

I remember my mom's face: I had forgotten that her seeing me like this was her biggest fear too.

"Matt, what is going on? You were already inside."

"I couldn't do it!" I screamed back at her. She kept asking me what was going on and trying to talk to me. All I could do was scream, "Don't make me do it! Don't make me go inside!"

My mom, who worked at a different school, had to leave. I was making her late for her job. Even though she did everything she could to get me back in school that day, I wouldn't budge. Eventually, she gave up and drove me home. I felt relieved but also guilty.

The next day, we tried again: I walked to the school doors, turned around, and screamed and hyperventilated until I could go home. The cycle repeated every day.

My mom and brothers tried to help me find ways around it. I stopped exiting the car as soon as we pulled up to school. Instead, I would sit there until I was ready to walk in. My mom also stopped driving away. Instead, she'd wait in the parking lot for as long as it took: sometimes 10 minutes, sometimes an hour. Some days, I'd approach the door after 15 minutes of sitting in the car, only to turn around and need an extra five minutes with my mom.

While this worked in the short term, it wasn't a solution. On the bright side, I was getting into the school, but at the same time, I was making my mom over an hour late to work. Plus, I was a stranger to my homeroom because I never made it on time, and my absences and tardiness made me fall behind in all of my classes. I may have been physically making it into the building, but the effort wasn't enough. I had to start going for the full day, I had to pass my classes, and my mom had to go to work.

My mom kept driving me to school while I kept trying to build up the courage to walk in. Every day, I made her late for work. *Every day.*

I kept trying and trying. Part of me felt horrible, but part of me felt numb. I knew that I was making life harder for her, but any other option seemed impossible.

After weeks of the same routine, I finally tried to walk to school with my brothers, and being with them actually worked better than I thought it would. We started walking, just making small conversation about the days before, like we always would. They asked me how I was doing, I told them, and they listened. We talked about our friends (who were really more their friends than mine) and when they all planned to hang out.

The walk was going great. But then, as we continued up the street, I started to see my school in the distance. The closer I got, the bigger the pit in my stomach got. I realized that when I walked to school, I still had the free will to turn around and go home, but once I entered the building, the only way I could leave was if my mom or dad dismissed me. Basically, the second I stepped into the building, there would be no leaving until seven and a half hours passed.

I thought back to my therapy sessions. Jessie told me I needed to test myself, but knowing how that went last time at the grocery store, I didn't want to try again. And I already wasn't with my mom. That was a huge step in itself. If I made it into school as well, that would be *two* huge steps in the right direction. So, that's what I did. I tested myself and walked right into school with my brothers.

What Hurts?

When I'm trying my best not to focus on my stomach, I tend to get lost in my head. I don't listen to the people or noise around me.

I just zone out.

A numbness overtook me every time I stepped into school. Class time, for me, meant staring at walls or posters. I resumed my habit of clicking all of the lead out of my mechanical pencils and then pushing it back in. Over and over again, the same thing.

The only time that I didn't zone out was when Ms. Summers was there. In my extra help class, Ms. Summers, the best teacher I ever had, sat down with me. Out of every teacher in the school, she understood me. She would sometimes pop into my English or math classes to ask me if I was doing okay, and she taught me lessons one-on-one.

"You're not doing the best in your classes," she said to me gently, trying to find the root of the problem.

"I know," I said. "I can't bring myself to focus on anything. My mind will race, and I'll go into a panic."

My explanation began with Jessie, how I was still going to therapy, but it wasn't working. To be honest, I kept going only because I had hope that, one day, something would click while I was talking with Jessie. I went into how I hated walking into buildings and that I didn't feel like myself in certain places outside of the house. I told Ms. Summers that it felt like my body was going to school, but I wasn't. The only time I felt like myself in school was in my extra help class. Then, I talked about school, the so-called progress that I had made, and my life. Ms. Summers tried to tell me how much better I was getting, and I guess she was right about some things. But whenever adults talked to me about "progress," I would think they were just saying that to make me feel better about myself, not because it was actually true.

Even if I couldn't fully accept what she was saying, Ms. Summers supported me in the one way I needed most: She made me feel like it was normal that I was having trouble. She didn't make me feel like I was going crazy. Without her even knowing it, she was doing more than Jessie ever did—because she was living the stressful moments *with* me. Jessie could only hear the stories after the fact, way later.

We had been in school for about a month and a half at this point. Everyone else seemed to be growing accustomed to seventh-grade life . . . but I had already used all four of my bathroom passes. Despite knowing this, I still asked Mr. G if I could use the bathroom, to which he replied, "You use the bathroom way too much."

My extra help teacher, thankfully, stopped him from making a scene in front of the class. She explained that he needed to let me take breaks. Even though he hated that she was right, he let me go. But my relationship with him only grew more distressing over time. Ms. Summers wasn't always around, and in those moments, Mr. G would be more strict about the bathroom pass rule. His ego wouldn't let him relax on any class policy, not when there was a chance a student could be using the bathroom pass to skip. Not on his watch.

Ms. Summers was the reason I had more than four bathroom passes in that class, but even she had moments of tough love. She wouldn't let me escape to the bathroom *all* of the time.

I may not have been the smartest kid when it came to schoolwork, but when it came to getting myself out of anxious situations, I was an *expert.*

Instead of spending time studying for tests, I studied the building: The school had three floors, a main entrance on the first floor, and an emergency exit down the hallway and past the secretary's and nurse's offices. The second floor had an exit in the stairwell, past the double doors to the wing where all of my classes were, and the stairwell also gave me a way up to the third floor. I had an escape plan for every hallway or classroom I stepped foot in. And if you didn't know me, you would think I built the building from the ground up because I memorized the layout so well.

I was also smart enough to realize that, yes, Mr. G could have his little bathroom rule and could stop me from going there, but there was absolutely nothing he could do if I asked to go to the nurse's office. Sure, he could have said, "You don't look sick," or, "What hurts? You don't look like you're in pain." But occasionally, a fake cough, a grab of a limb, and maybe if I was feeling a little risky, a fake limp, really helped me get away with just about anything.

The whole "in pain" act worked for me a little too well. Whenever I got an anxiety attack in the middle of the day, I would simply ask to go to the nurse's office and stand in the private bathroom there for 30 minutes straight, or sometimes for so long that I would lose track of what class I was supposed to be in. In those cases, I would just leave whenever another student knocked on the door. The funniest part of this was that, even though I went to the nurse's office so often, I never actually saw the nurse. I didn't need her for any health-related problems; I only went so I could be alone.

All of this worked for me, but only on days when I actually made it into the school.

Eventually, I ran into problems getting into the building again. My mom still drove herself to work every day while I was supposed to be walking to school with my brothers.

But it didn't take long for the routine to fall apart.

Matthew O. Sturniolo
Birth Date: 8/1/2003

Chief Complaint

- Anxiety
- Attention-deficit hyperactivity disorder
- Academic problems

History of Present Illness

Pt noted his anxiety at school has decreased a lot. He is more able to concentrate on his school work, due to not feeling so anxious. He walked to school with his brothers one day and has gone into the school by himself.

Discussed how to manage his worries about meeting up with his brothers and walking home alone. Discussed how to change unhelpful thoughts to helpful thoughts. Praised Pt for his efforts.

Target Symptom: Anxiety

- Frequency: Sometimes
- Intensity: Moderate
- Status: Improved

Target Symptom: School Attendance

- Frequency: Never
- Intensity: Absent
- Status: Improved

Skills Taught/Reinforced

- Expressing thoughts/feelings
- Grounding techniques
- Identifying dysfunctional thoughts/behaviors
- Rational self-talk
- Distraction methods

A+

Why Would They Torture Themselves?

I showered first every morning because, according to my brothers, it took me the longest to get ready, even though I never felt like I was moving that slow.

One day, when I finished putting on my clothes, brushing my teeth, and doing all the normal stuff everyone does before leaving the house, I laid down on the couch, waited for Nick and Chris, and ended up falling asleep. Once they were ready to head out, they tried to wake me up and convince me to walk with them. But I refused. Instead, they left without me, and I waited until the last possible moment to start my trek to school. My brothers loved to show up early because they would eat breakfast in the cafeteria with their friends, but I couldn't get behind the idea of being in the school building for a minute longer than necessary. If that's what they wanted to do, I wouldn't stop them from torturing themselves.

The school was only an eight-minute walk. I set my phone alarm to 10 minutes before I had to be in my first class, woke up, and tried to be right out the door. If I walked fast enough, I knew I would be at my desk right in time. However, I failed to account for the panic attacks I would endure walking by myself.

The further and further I got away from my house, the more the pit in my stomach grew and the heavier my breathing became. Now, I was alone, not walking with Nick and Chris and not being dropped off by my mom. The decision to go to school was mine. No one stood beside me, encouraging me to approach the doors and step in.

I turned around, and I was gone, running straight home.

The more I ran, the better (but also the more confused) I felt. The guilt set in when I thought about my brothers sitting at lunch, disappointed when they didn't see me there too, and Ms. Summers looking for me in my classes, only to realize I wasn't there to say, "Here!" during attendance. Part of me felt horrible, but another part of me felt so free: I would only go to school on my terms, and I would walk away whenever I wanted to.

For that whole week, I tried to make it before the first bell rang, but I would stop at the sidewalk in front of the school, look at the building, and sprint home. Some days, I would make it back to our front porch and, while putting the key in our front door to go inside, I would try to encourage myself to walk back to school and try again. But I never would. Other days, when I would go back to my house, I only stayed for a while to sleep a little longer, and then I'd drag myself to school around lunchtime.

I was on my own schedule.

Who Could I Be?

No one ever sat me down and explained the potential side effects or even what the medication was supposed to do. All I remember is that one morning, before I went to school, a pill bottle appeared on the kitchen table, filled with what we called "Matt's little red pills." Much later, I found out that I was taking Concerta. I may have only been on it for about a year, but for over a decade afterward, I never knew the name of it, although I had a couple of guesses.

I started to hate my therapist for her decision to prescribe me this stuff. Jessie had recommended to my doctor that I be on medication for my focus. It felt like an easy way out. A lot of my feelings went numb on the meds, and a huge part of me vanished. And instead of thinking that the medicine was causing side effects, I started thinking, "Oh, there must be something wrong with *me*. I must be going crazy."

The worst part was the inconsistency. Some days, I would feel the best I've ever felt in my whole life. The pills made going to school a tiny bit easier, and I was suddenly able to attend class. I would go to school with my brothers, laughing, having fun, stopping at the convenience store on the way to buy snacks for lunch, and even walking with them to friends' houses after school. I was doing the things that I hadn't been comfortable doing for about a year and a half. But of course, it was easy because, thanks to the meds, I didn't feel fear. Actually, I didn't feel anything. No stress, no panic, no anxiety. I just existed.

On the pills, I'd sometimes completely disassociate, almost as if I fell asleep while standing up with my eyes open in broad daylight. My thoughts were consumed by the medication. I could only focus on how the pills were inside of my body, or I would create scenarios of who I was without them. So much time was spent imagining who I *could* be without the pills, without anxiety at all. Rather than let me pay attention in class and learn better, it felt like the pills only opened a new way of overthinking, so much so that I'd stare blankly at random objects and posters in my classes or daydream for entire periods. These random feelings of nothing would last for I don't even know how long; that's how much I detached from reality. The highs were high, but the lows were lower than before.

This is when I put my master plan of skipping class into full effect. Well, it wasn't actually a big master plan, but I needed to find a way to escape without making it anyone else's problem anymore.

Two circumstances made my getaway possible. One: When my grandpa moved to Massachusetts from Portugal decades ago, he bought all of his family members houses, so he and my grandmother, my uncles, my mom and dad, me, and my brothers lived in the same neighborhood, close to each other and the school. Two: The careless school nurse could have had her job stolen by a mini fridge because all she ever did was hand out ice packs. I had the hardest time being at school after lunch, with the end of the school day being so close but so far away. Some days, when I couldn't take the anxiety anymore, I would ask the school nurse for a pass so I could "get fresh air" outside. The pass was not much more than a sheet where you filled out your classroom number, your name, and where you were going—it almost looked like a slip of paper a waiter would use to take your order.

I wasn't lying when I said I needed fresh air; I just extended the time outside more than I was supposed to. I would take the pass she gave me to the second floor, walk past all the classrooms I was supposed to be in, and go into the stairwell with the double doors. Then, as soon as the doors to the stairwell closed behind me and no one could see me, I shot through the side door exit and ran to my grandma's house.

No time was wasted; I could make it from the school to her backyard in three minutes—the same backyard where me and my brothers played football as kids and where my grandpa bought a swingset for us. The swingset, now a bit torn up and rusted, still sat in the corner of the yard. And it is still there today. Each time I ran there, I would sit on a swing, look up at the sky, and breathe. The crazy part was I always had a pit in my stomach, and I would still have anxiety attacks simply because I wasn't home. But for some reason, the attacks seemed more manageable in the yard. The thrill of being out of school may have made my anxiety peak again, but in a weird way, it almost felt comforting. Because of my pills, I had felt nothing for so long that the pit in my stomach felt familiar. Normal. My grandma's yard became the only place where I could feel like myself again.

I would kick my feet back and forth on the swing until the fear—of my grandma coming home and catching me or of someone at school noticing I was gone—would make me hurry back to class. To enter the school through the side door, I had to wait for someone else to exit through it, and then I could find my class and show my teacher the outside pass. I ditched school for my grandma's backyard about nine times, only stopping because the last time I did it, a full 20 minutes passed before someone let me in the side door, and I barely caught the last 10 minutes of my final class. Somehow, no one grilled me about why it took half an hour (at minimum) to "get fresh air."

Matthew O. Sturniolo
Birth Date: 8/1/2003

Chief Complaint
- Anxiety
- Attention-deficit hyperactivity disorder
- Academic problems

History of Present Illness
Mom shared that Pt started Concerta. She noted that his math teacher notices a difference in Pt's ability to focus since starting the medication. Pt does not feel he needs the medication. He feels the changes are due to his efforts and not the medication.

Discussed stopping the medication for a time, with doctor's permission, to see if Pt is able to demonstrate effort on his own. Mom would like to continue the medication and talk to all of his teachers to see if they notice a difference.

Encouraged Pt to trust the adults on what they see. Mom noted she will let Pt ultimately make the decision about taking medication or not.

Pt was not very talkative and did not appear himself in the session. He did note he has no anxiety in the morning, at school, or after school. Mom reported that he is doing great. Pt said he has a little anxiety but was not able to say more.

Pt feels he is ready to be done with therapy. Mom will keep in touch with therapist about making another appointment, if needed.

Target Symptom: Anxiety
- Frequency: Seldom
- Intensity: Slight
- Status: Improved

Target Symptom: School Attendance
- Frequency: Never
- Intensity: Absent
- Status: Improved

Skills Taught/Reinforced
- Expressing thoughts/feelings
- Grounding techniques
- Rational self-talk
- Parenting strategies
- Problem-solving

How Do I Make It to Class?

I had no more games to play. My grades were still horrible, and my attendance was very, very rocky. Everyone, from my teachers to my parents to my brothers, was locked onto me, offering me endless solutions on how to make it to class. With how hands-on my mom was, plus how connected Ms. Summers was to the faculty, there were likely many behind-the-scenes conversations about my attendance that I never heard. My teachers even made it nearly impossible for me to fail their classes, giving all of the assignments I missed to my brothers so I could do them later and offering to let me stay after school to catch up on work. Nearly all of them approached me at one point or another to tell me which mornings they were free before school if I wanted to come in early and get a head start. And don't get me wrong; the work and concern my teachers put in *would* have made school so much easier—if only I could cross the entrance to the building. The problem kept persisting until, one day, getting into the building wasn't my choice at all.

Pulling up to school one morning, my mom parked in front of the main entrance rather than the side door like normal. She had decided to drive me to school again to ensure that I made it into the building, and she spent the entire drive rooting for me and hyping me up, telling me how I could do it and that once I passed through the doors, I would be okay; I just needed to put the effort into getting inside. She wasn't wrong. Walking in was the hardest part for me.

I made the smallest effort possible by opening the car door, sticking my feet out, and staring at the school's metal doors, which, according to my mind, may as well have been jail bars.

"You got it," my mom cheered. "Go ahead."

Just like last time and the time before that, I hopped out of the car and tried my best to walk in, but then I panicked as a pit formed in my stomach. I did a 180-degree spin and darted for the car door handle, swinging open the backseat and crying into my hands. The same broken record.

He tries to go to school but doesn't.

He tries to go outside but can't.

Over and over again.

Everyone was so sick of it: me, my brothers, my friends, my teachers, and my parents. As I looked up at the building again with tears in my eyes, I saw Ms. Summers and my school's vice principal, Mr. Conway, walking straight at me.

"Come on, Matt. Let's go," Ms. Summers said through the glass window. "You can do it."

Mr. Conway didn't say a word; he just watched my mom and Ms. Summers pass words of encouragement back and forth. He put his hands on his hips and kept a straight face. Knowing we all wanted the same simple thing, I started crying even harder. I was the only reason everyone was awkwardly standing outside my mom's minivan. To make the situation even better, just about every kid in my grade looked at me weird while walking by or, worse, stood and stared while talking to their friends. Well, until first period started and the bell rang. The kids were then rushed inside by teachers, the doors slamming shut behind them.

"Look, this is the perfect time to sneak in and blend in with the crowd. It will be nice and easy," Ms. Summers pointed out.

I cried some more and screamed my classic anxiety attack catchphrase, "I can't do it! Don't make me do it!" Leave it to me to find a way to make everyone feel even more guilty.

When I started to hyperventilate, my mom told me to breathe and rubbed my back, and the adults surrounding me waited a little longer for me to catch my breath. Once I seemed to regain my composure, Mr. Conway stepped in.

"Alright, let's go," he said, grabbing my wrists. I quickly jerked my hands away, tucking them close to my chest, under my armpits. But that's when Ms. Summers locked her hands around my ankles. I tried to pull my feet away.

This is what I mean when I say "Matt's little red pill" created higher highs and lower lows. As Mr. Conway and Ms. Summers hoisted me up, my mind went blank. I screamed and cried, and while I closed my eyes and flailed my limbs, I can't remember who, but Mr. Conway or Ms. Summers definitely caught a good kick. My mom watched from her seat with tears in her eyes, knowing that I may have been upset, but force was the only way to get me in school they hadn't tried yet. She recalls this day as one of her saddest memories of my anxiety. It tore her up having to see me in so much pain.

A minute passed before they regained control of my arms and legs. The fact that I could hold them off for that long was an accomplishment, considering I was such a small, light kid. They dragged me out of the car, picked me up by my limbs, and carried me into the school like a ragdoll. They even tried to lug me up the stairs, but at the first step, I stopped screaming and told them I would walk the rest of the way. Even though I never stopped freaking out, I didn't want to embarrass myself anymore.

Once they put me down, Mr. Conway headed to his office downstairs, but he looked back at me to see if I would try to run out once he turned away. Ms. Summers, not wanting me to face a room full of teenagers with tears still in my eyes, took me to the guidance counselor's office to see Mrs. Casey, who, unlike Ms. Summers, was never any real help to me at all.

Matthew O. Sturniolo
Birth Date: 8/1/2003

Chief Complaint

- Anxiety
- Attention-deficit hyperactivity disorder
- Academic problems

History of Present Illness

Mom feels Pt's medication is beginning to work. He appears and reports that he is less anxious.

Pt wants to start sharing his experience with anxiety with his friends, so if it happens again, he won't feel as embarrassed. Discussed being aware of this choice to tell his story, but also that what matters most is what he thinks of himself. Discussed moving toward giving this experience less power.

Pt continues to feel that his experience with anxiety makes up one-fourth of who he is.

Mom reported they will be transferring to another therapist—one who takes their insurance. Discussed things to continue to work on with his next therapist. Discussed that Pt is welcome to return if needed.

Target Symptom: Anxiety

- Frequency: Always
- Intensity: Severe
- Status: Worsened

Target Symptom: School Attendance

- Frequency: Never
- Intensity: Absent
- Status: Improved

Skills Taught/Reinforced

- Expressing thoughts/feelings
- Grounding techniques
- Rational self-talk

Diagnosis

- Generalized anxiety disorder

Will You Stop Freaking Out?

"Why did you have trouble walking into school today?" Mrs. Casey asked. Just like when Jessie asked me why I thought I had anxiety attacks, the question angered me. Again, if I knew the answer to that question, I wouldn't be having the problem, would I?

"I don't know. I always do," I replied.

Mrs. Casey shook the bowl of salad she packed for lunch, completely interrupting any conversation she hoped to start. She proceeded to tell me the importance of eating before starting your day, and as usual, she talked about herself for what seemed like an eternity before pestering me with more questions and theories:

"Hmm . . . Let's see. Why could this be hard for you?"

"You're probably nervous about your grades."

"You can always find solutions."

Blah, blah, blah.

I never said a single word during what was supposed to be a two-way conversation. Instead, she could have talked to herself for hours about nothing, to the point where I wondered if I left, would she even notice—or would she continue talking to the wall behind me?

Once I calmed down, without any help from her, she wrote me a pass to class, which is exactly where I went. I attended every class that day, but I just felt numb. Defeated. No matter how hard I tried, I could not find a way out, and I had to accept that. Even as more days went by, I continued to show up to school and complete my work with Ms. Summers, who didn't bring me to the guidance counselor anymore after I explained how unhelpful she was. Instead, I would just talk to Ms. Summers. This is when my days started to become the tiniest bit better. Some days, forcing myself through the school doors was excruciating, but I coached myself through it because I would have rather walked in than be rag-dolled again.

The only remaining problem was . . . the person going to school and finishing his work wasn't me. He was a red-pilled, medicated zombie with no emotions—no sadness, no fear, no anger, no joy. Just a body wandering around, listening to people tell him where to go and what to do next. The emotions would only return when my meds wore off. I would have moments of clarity where, even if I felt bad, at least I would also feel normal again.

When I realized this, I told my mom that I would never take that medication again, and I wanted to stop seeing Jessie. My mom, being a mom, saw I wasn't acting like myself, and she knew how much help Ms. Summers was to me. So she agreed to let me cut out the medicine and Jessie. Quitting therapy was a big risk for me to take, but I think even my mom was tired of hearing the same story every week, just in a different font.

I wouldn't learn until much later that therapy only works if you *accept* you're going to therapy. Being forced into it won't do anything; you have to want your life to change.

My mom encouraged my older brother, Justin, to go to therapy when he was a freshman in high school. Justin would go, but he hated his therapist and didn't think it worked. And when I talked to him about it, he said, "Oh, yeah. I just lied to my therapist the entire time I was there."

Not seeing Jessie anymore was a relief to young me because I just wasn't ready yet, and I didn't want to be there. Looking back, I'm glad I was introduced to it and encouraged by my mom, but at that point, when I left Jessie, I assumed I was never going back to therapy again.

While dropping therapy was one thing, the medication was another. What would happen when I released the floodgates and could feel every emotion again? At the slightest inconvenience, would I feel every emotion all at once and have a total meltdown? Would going off the pills make all my progress disappear? Was I ready for that?

After thinking about every possible outcome, I came to the conclusion that taking away my moments of happiness, just so I didn't have to feel sad, would never be worth it. After that day, I never saw Jessie or that little red pill again, and I went back to feeling like myself again almost instantly. The anxiety was still there, but I was still getting to school and even staying after the bell rang to improve my grades. Though, obviously, the absence of medication didn't magically change my life. I still had days when I would rot away in the nurse's office, days when I would sleep in, and days when I would show up late. But I *saw* real progress for the first time, instead of hearing the adults in my life reassure me I was making progress over and over—something I never believed.

Chris and Nick saw the progress too. I may have still been freaking out, but they saw action being taken to help me, whether it be from my mom or Ms. Summers. As brothers, they helped in their own ways. If we were at the grocery store and I was feeling anxious, Nick would yell at me to calm down, while Chris would calmly break down my surroundings to focus me on the present.

Nick would scream, "Matt! Will you stop *freaking out*? Jesus! Stop being so dramatic."

"Matt. We're in the grocery store. The exit is *right* there. Our car is in the parking lot. We're a five-minute drive from the house. If you need a bathroom, there is one," Chris would follow up. "You're going to be fine."

The good cop, bad cop routine may have never helped me stop losing it, but at least I knew I had people who cared about me.

What About Fluoxetine?

My anxiety after stopping Concerta was hard to figure out.

Before the pill, everything set me off: school, friends' houses, the supermarket, sports practices, and games. Legit anywhere other than my house.

While taking the pill, I didn't feel *as* anxious as before, but that's because I didn't *feel* anything. My emotions were gone, so technically, I was gone.

But after the pill, everything felt so random and unpredictable. School would be easy one minute, but then the worst place ever the next. I wouldn't think about how stressed I was for hours, but then suddenly, I'd have the thought, *I can't do this anymore. I hate it here.*

My anxiety and relationship with medicine were further complicated by a trip to the doctor around the time I ended therapy with Jessie.

"What would you think about going on fluoxetine?" the doctor asked.

I immediately hated the idea. I never wanted to take pills for my anxiety again.

I later shared my concern with the doctor and my mom, but everyone disagreed. When you google "fluoxetine" (a.k.a. Prozac), the first few search results say it "treats depression, anxiety, and panic attacks," i.e., exactly what I have. The last pill I took was supposedly for ADHD, which was the wrong problem, so I started to think that maybe fluoxetine would actually work. Taking it might affect me differently since it would actually target the right issue.

I caved in. Like last time, one 10 milligram tablet appeared on the kitchen table every morning, and I took it. I don't know if the doctor was ever told that I wasn't going to therapy with Jessie anymore, but still, the pills showed up.

Anxiety wasn't new to my mom. She had suffered from anxiety as a child, often telling her mom, "I can't breathe." She *could* breathe, but what she really meant was she couldn't take a deep breath. Her anxious thoughts kept her breathing shallow. She's told me that there's a joke that Portuguese people are all nervous, and her aunts in the old country would often write letters to her mother about their "agonias," which translates to stress or anxiety. Having taken Prozac herself, my mom thought if the issue wasn't ADHD and focus, maybe a medication to tackle the anxiety might help me.

No noticeable difference happened because of the Prozac though. I kept going to school and having the same thoughts as before. Obviously, I didn't think this new pill would instantly cure me of all negative thoughts and feelings, but it also wasn't hurting anything. I continued taking it every morning, waiting for the day it actually did something.

Some days, I would skip school but still walk to friends' houses with Nick and Chris, and we'd walk all around our neighborhoods and the city. The next day, I would think about how it was unbelievable I did all of that and how I would never leave my house again. Long story short, it was hard for me to predict my anxiety, so it was even harder for everyone else to predict it too. The only thing we all knew for sure was that I *would* eventually get anxious about something, even if we didn't know when.

The uncertainty scared me.

My anxiety went from being constant (and familiar) to something completely unhinged and wild.

Email Sent: 2/15/2016
Contact: PCP
Purpose of Contact: Clinical Matter

Hi Jessie,

I'm Matt Sturniolo's pediatrician. I saw him last week in a follow-up evaluation for his ADHD medication, during which time the degree of his anxiety was acknowledged alongside your concern (as related by his mother) that Matt might be a candidate for treatment for his anxiety.

In our visit last Tuesday, that certainly seemed the case. On the "SCARED" form, he scored quite positive for social anxiety disorder. He actually seemed quite depressed during his examination.

Despite feedback from his teachers that he has been doing much better academically when he's taking stimulant medications, he pretty much refused its use, indicating that he feels like he's "cheating" when he's taking the Concerta. Interestingly, he readily agreed to take fluoxetine for his anxiety, and I went ahead and started him on a very low dose of that medication.

I'll be seeing him next week for a medical follow-up, and I'm very pleased that you'll be seeing him regularly during this time. I'd appreciate any feedback that you might be able to offer.

Nathan

I have been surrounded by sports for as long as I can remember, and hockey (second to football) was a big deal in our town, with TD Garden being close by and students and parents showing up to all the varsity games. Even though me, Nick, and Chris were so close and did everything together during the early parts of our lives, especially as pre-teens, I really looked up to Justin. When I saw him playing sports and video games or even getting his driver's license, I saw my future. I was introduced to baseball, hockey, and lacrosse through him. When he was in seventh grade, I was a toddler walking around the baseball field, and in the wintertime, I would watch him play hockey from the bleachers, not knowing I'd be on the ice one day too.

Despite how familiar sports were to me and how much I used to love playing, everything changed for me after that day of baseball. I didn't view sports as fun anymore, not like I did before. Now, practices were a task I had to complete to get home again.

Me and Chris had been playing hockey for a couple of years, and in the beginning, I really did love it. I originally got into it by going to Justin's practices or learning how to free skate at our local rink, not even playing the game until I reached a certain age. Nick tried doing the same thing once and absolutely hated it. But the same way I watched Justin play and envisioned myself doing that, Nick had that moment watching me and Chris, so he decided to play during our seventh-grade year. Me and Chris already had years of experience before Nick, so we were a little better than he was and weren't surprised when Nick had to play on a lower-level team. (We were on the AA team, but Nick was just on the A.)

That season, our lives outside of school were practically dedicated to hockey, which was hard for me because I loved it, but the anxiety hit pretty hard. With Nick being on a different team, our practice schedule may have been the same, but our games were either on different days or hours after each other.

Despite both my brothers often being close by, even making it on the ice was a challenge. I would put on the shin pads, the socks, the pants, and the skates, but when it came to putting on the chest pad, I hated it. Pulling the velcro tight above my waist, my stomach would sink and feel empty, like I had just put on a straitjacket. Feeling trapped, I started to find any way I could to avoid it—the same thing I did with everything in my life that gave me anxious thoughts.

I would strap on all of my pads, and then once I put my jersey on, I would reach under it and unstrap the chest pad. Without the chest pad being skin tight, I couldn't hold my stick, pass, or shoot right, but everything that I did came second to my anxiety. I didn't care if I had the worst shot or pass on the team.

Unsurprisingly, I had my first anxiety attack during hockey season while putting on the pads. The more I put on, the more anxious I got. The heavy gear made me feel claustrophobic, like I was suffocating. If I wanted to go home, not only would it be a 12-minute drive, but I would also have to take off three layers of equipment, which would take five whole minutes, if not more. And I couldn't exactly run down the street with hockey blades on my feet.

Even though Chris was there to calm me down, the anxiety only grew worse over time. Before hockey season, I felt okay for the rest of the day when school ended, especially if I decided to go home instead of to friends' houses. But now, I had to enter the hockey rink too. My anxiety attacks doubled.

As you can imagine, dropping me off at practice didn't work like it did for the other players. Pulling up to the rink, kids never wanted to carry the heavy bags of equipment through the parking lot and inside, so the parents would drop them off at the front or back of the building and then park the car, carrying all of the gear themselves. But for me, just like with school, I would pull all of my stuff out of the car, walk to the door, watch my mom start to inch away toward the parking lot, and run back to the car, crying and screaming.

The same way I was searching for solutions in school was now a part of hockey. And just like school, we eventually worked out a system to push me through the doors.

Chris would bring my hockey bag and stick into the rink, I would go with my mom to park the car, and my mom would walk me to the locker rooms. At least one major difference from school made hockey easier: My mom could come into the rink. A lot of parents would sit in the warm room, do work, and talk while the practice was going on, so it wasn't weird for her to stay . . . until I made it weird by asking her to sit on the bleachers, where I could see her, instead of in the warm room like the other parents.

My mom would sit on the bleachers in a puffy jacket, working on her iPad with one glove off so she could touch the screen. Part of me felt guilty—it was my fault that she had to sit in the cold for no reason other than I wanted to be able to see her.

The days when Mom had meetings at night and could only drop us off were the hardest. Chris would make me comfortable enough to get into the building, but once I was skating around on the ice and couldn't see my mom, the panic would set in again. Skating fast and losing my breath didn't help because my brain associated heavy, fast breathing with anxiety attacks. Then, when I would look up and not see my mom, I would skate off the ice without asking my coach, head straight to the locker room, and take off the upper half of my equipment so I could breathe without feeling like there was a 100-pound weight on my chest. It wasn't enough to sit on the bench and wait out the attack; I had to physically remove myself from everyone else. I would call my mom, and she either wouldn't answer because she was in her meeting or she would answer and calm me down, telling me that practice would only last for a little bit longer.

Sometimes it felt much longer than I could handle, but it was easy enough for me to slip away. I wasn't a star player on the team, so me sneaking off wasn't much of a distraction. Especially when the rest of the players were dealing with a certain practice coach. The coach for our team was a great guy, but sometimes all the teams would practice together. When that happened, we'd have an especially strict coach run the practice, and he was *intense*. If kids were hitting each other with sticks while they were skating, the coach would throw his stick as hard as he could, straight at the glass. One time, he found out a player was dating his daughter, and that player had to practice skating way more than everyone else. Luckily, no one noticed when I skated off the ice for a break.

Chris was the only reason I could still play. If he didn't, I would have quit. And I could never have been in the same position as Nick, who played without anyone he knew and had to make friends on his own. I started to look forward to hearing what Nick had to say about his team, especially glad that he was enjoying it because, if I were in his shoes, I would have been a wreck.

More time went by with the same routine, but soon, my brothers mixed it up. Every day we came home from school and hockey, they started talking more and more about this kid, Nathan, on Nick's hockey team.

Nathan was a good passer and team player, one of the best on the team, and his parents loved watching him play. The only reason he was on Nick's team (the A team) was because he was a year younger than us. It was difficult to be friends with some people because all they thought or talked about was a certain sport, and they were under such an insane amount of pressure to succeed. But not Nathan. His dad, Pat, may have been a crazy strict hockey dad, but he only loved the sport so much because Nathan did too.

I'll never forget the time when, during a game, Nathan's mom and dad were in total concentration watching their son play, and Nick begged our mom, "Can you go stand next to them so that you guys can be friends too? So that we can all be friends?"

Our mom walked over to Pat and started chatting with him in a very funny, very awkward way. Pat the Sports Dad was so focused on Nathan that you could tell all he wanted to do was watch the game, but our mom could have sat there all day, just talking. It wasn't lost on me that Nick had asked our mom to go up and make friends with one of the best player's parents.

Soon after that, Nick made plans to go to Nathan's house. In the middle of a snowstorm.

I went with my mom to drop off Nick at Nathan's house. Ice covered the roads, and we started to think that Nick may have to sleep over, not sure that we could make it back out to Nathan's house in the crazy weather. Later that night, after my mom drove us home safely, we waited for the snow to stop and for the plows to clear the streets. When we picked up Nick, Nathan and his mom were waving goodbye from the doorway, and Nick had an instant, huge smile on his face. He looked back at me and Chris from the passenger seat and told us everything.

"His room is Bruins-themed with yellow and black walls. He has a huge dog. We rode around his kitchen on his green hoverboard and then did crafts with his little brother. His cousins came over, and we played Minecraft all day." Without stopping for a breath, he explained every detail to us, told my mom more about Nathan's parents, and told me and Chris that we had to go next time.

I eventually met Nathan and his family after Nick's games, and we became friends just by going to team dinners and events. But I still couldn't go to his house with Nick and Chris. Even though getting into school had become easier by this point, I still struggled to go over to friends' houses. At least, with school, I was familiar with the routine, but going to a friend's house was different. While I knew our school was only an eight-minute walk home, we had friends all over the city. Their houses could have been any distance away from ours, and I wouldn't risk not being able to run home whenever I wanted. Absolutely not happening.

For the longest time, whenever my mom dropped us off, I begged her to keep her phone within arm's reach. And when that stopped working—either because she needed to use her phone for work calls or, honestly, because she lost her phone a lot—I asked her to park across the street from my friends' houses. She would work outside in the car, and I'd hang out inside, looking out the window at her car instead of socializing. My friends would start conversations, but I'd zone out and miss what they said, too busy watching my mom talk on the phone outside.

But my mom wasn't sitting outside in her car for me anymore, mostly since I felt guilty and stopped making her do it. Now, I couldn't look at her every time I felt a pit in my stomach.

It also depended on the friend's parents. Would they be understanding of my anxiety? Would they be okay with me leaving at a moment's notice because I didn't feel comfortable in their home? With outings that were farther away, like the movies, I never risked going to something I couldn't easily get out of. I didn't want to have to call my mom or dad to pick me up because, sometimes, that wasn't an option.

Nathan's house was anything but walking distance. It was all the way across the city. And while I wanted to go so badly and saw how I was missing out, I also knew that I'd struggled to go to friends' houses for years, and I just couldn't bring myself to go with them. Trapping me in a stranger's house miles away from my own home with no simple exit strategy seemed like a terrible idea.

After about a month and a half of school days and hockey nights, Nick and Chris planned to go over to Nathan's house again, and somehow, this time, I worked up the courage to go with them. My brothers loved his family; plus, I had built more trust with Nathan's parents because of hockey. Nervous but determined, I talked myself into it, and the next day, my mom dropped all of us off.

I met the giant dog Nick was talking about. We played knee hockey in his room with miniature sticks and nets. His dad ordered us pizza, and we ate dinner together. I couldn't believe how easy it was, probably the easiest being at a friend's house had ever been in my entire life. His mom and dad were generous and caring, and Nathan was a nice kid—a little shy like me, but that didn't stop him from making me feel welcome. Even though he was on Nick's team and had known him for longer, he still treated me and Chris just the same. He even let his little brother join our hockey games and eat pizza with us.

When our mom came to pick us up later, the three of us started talking all at once, interrupting each other to excitedly tell our mom about all the fun we had.

"How was your time, Matt?" my mom turned her attention to me. "You had fun?"

I then told her about everything we did and how awesome it was. She smiled and listened to every detail. Even though I still wasn't perfect, she wanted me to celebrate the small wins just as much as the big ones.

Matthew O. Sturniolo
Birth Date: 8/1/2003

Chief Complaint

- Anxiety
- Attention-deficit hyperactivity disorder
- Academic problems

History of Present Illness

Mother and Pt came in first. Mother noted Pt's anxiety has increased significantly since returning to school after the holiday break.

Outside of school, Pt most often wants to be with a parent and/or know where they are. He used to go into hockey by himself but now needs his mom to go with him. Pt is not doing things he would like to do because he wants to be with a parent.

Pt noted he is worried about his entire family and, at first, could not identify a reason. Pt is at a 9 on the stress scale (1–10) on being worried about his family. Pt noted that he has been worried about his family for two years (since the incident at baseball), and his worries are getting worse. Pt struggled to talk and appeared very distressed.

Therapist brought mom in alone and discussed what was talked about with Pt. Therapist discussed that Pt's symptoms appear to be very significant, and medication management may be helpful at this time. Mom noted she has an appointment with Pt's PCP next week and will discuss medication with him. Mom noted Pt's anxiety was added to his IEP at school and will receive counseling at school.

Discussed Pt's grandfather dying two years ago around the same time as the baseball incident and the possible connection between these two events.

Target Symptom: Anxiety

- Frequency: Always
- Intensity: Severe
- Status: Worsened

Target Symptom: School Attendance

- Frequency: Never
- Intensity: Absent
- Status: Improved

Skills Taught/Reinforced

- Expressing thoughts/feelings
- Grounding techniques
- Rational self-talk
- Parenting strategies
- Problem-solving

Diagnosis

- Generalized anxiety disorder
- Ruled out separation anxiety disorder of childhood

CAND

A Second Family?

When Nathan heard that I had anxiety, he thought it was contagious like the flu, saying something like, "Oh, you caught that too?"

As hockey season continued, my family grew closer to Nathan's, and his family started to come to Chris's and my games as we did with Nick's and Nathan's. We were seeing each other all the time, and no one ever treated me differently because of my anxiety. Least of all Nathan, who I think just believed I was shy and related to that, being introverted himself.

My social anxiety got better as I started to spend my time with people who accepted me, and hockey became easier as time went on. That's why I enjoyed going to Nick's games and team events more than my own—because I'd finally be able to see friends like Nathan, who went to different schools. Plus, all the parents would come to team dinners with us, so my parents started forming bonds with Nathan's parents, making our group tighter.

Nathan's parents, Pat and Eileen, started understanding my anxiety as well, and they made sure I always felt comfortable. I began to trust them more and more, and they even drove me and Chris to hockey games, which I allowed because I knew if I needed to leave, they would drive me home just like my mom or dad would.

On days when my parents were working, I could call up Pat or Eileen if I had a problem. And every time I went over to their house, Pat would ask me if I wanted anything to drink and tell me never to hesitate to get anything I needed, and Eileen was so accepting of anyone and everyone who stepped through her doors. Being over there was different from our house in a lot of ways—but in good ways, which surprised me.

I think Nathan's little brother swore more at the age of seven than I did throughout all four years of high school. And unlike our house, there was never-ending pizza, soda, and candy within arm's reach. Actually, Pat is probably the reason that Chris is *still* addicted to soda and can kill an entire case in the span of a few hours. Also, it felt like every time we went to see Nathan, some cousin or other relative would be there that we'd never met before. His family was huge. We were so close that me, Nick, and Chris called *his* grandpa "Grandpa Dave."

My favorite thing was when my mom would come to pick us up. Any time she had to say goodbye to Pat, she would open her arms to him, a tough guy townie from Boston, and say, "Alright, c'mon, Pat. You gotta give me hugs!"

Pretty soon, Pat and Eileen became the first adults in my life, other than my parents, who felt safe. The only places where I didn't feel anxious were my home and, now, Nathan's house too.

Who's Goalie?

One weekend at his house, Nathan mentioned that Somerville was finally getting its own youth lacrosse team. The hockey season had ended, so I was back to focusing on school again. And while I didn't miss skating or playing, I did miss my friends from different schools, especially Nathan. We still saw each other once in a while, but not nearly as often.

None of us had played lacrosse before, minus Justin, who played it when he was younger as part of a team in a different city. I remember me and Chris going to his games and playing catch with the lacrosse sticks while Justin would talk to his friends. That was the only lacrosse experience either one of us had.

The idea of another sport in my schedule scared me. Since baseball, every day was different for me, but when I was on a team and playing sports, that's when I really felt *it* again: being on the other side of the fence, standing at the corner of the building, hyperventilating with nowhere to run. Still, I didn't want to miss out on life again because of my anxiety. If I hadn't tried something new, I would have never gotten close to what would become a second family for life. I was quickly learning that if I wanted to find happiness, I had to be comfortable with being uncomfortable.

My mom was good about never forcing me into something but encouraging me to at least try it. That way, I would know what I was up against. So, I made the decision to play lacrosse. I wasn't excited about it, but I knew I needed to give life and friends a try again. With Nate, Chris, and Nick all being on the same team as me, I would have been an idiot not to give lacrosse a chance. I just kept thinking, *This is how I get better*.

When we first showed up to lacrosse practice that spring, I was nervous at first because of my lack of experience, and I really didn't know much about how to be good at the sport. Most of the kids who played hockey were there, so I knew a lot of my teammates, but there were also new kids as well. I still wasn't confident enough to try and meet new people, so I stayed with my brothers and Nathan. The practice started with the coaches giving all the kids their pads, helmets, and jerseys, and then we did normal conditioning drills, just running cone to cone, line to line, and getting used to moving with the ball in the stick without dropping it. After we ran for about 15 minutes, the coaches told us to start working on drills for our positions.

Lacrosse was immediately and obviously different from any other sport I'd played. In lacrosse, there are 10 players from each team on the field at a time: three defense, three attack, three middies, and one goalie. Nobody had really played before, so people didn't know what positions to choose. The fast kids figured they'd be middies since they had to run back and forth across the full field for the entire game—which is why I knew that wouldn't be my position. If I played as a middie with anxiety, my fast breathing would turn into hyperventilating, which would cause a panic attack the same way it did when I played hockey. I guess it's also worth noting that I have asthma, which has never been super serious but definitely didn't help.

As much as I didn't want to be a middie, I also didn't want to play attack either, since those were the strongest, best-shooting kids who had the most opportunities to score. And if you weren't one of those two positions, then you automatically fell into defense, which was fine with me. I was a defenseman in hockey, so that was the position I was most interested in.

"Alright, everybody. Who's going to be our goalie?" the coach asked, looking to the net and then back at the kids.

I thought for sure the guy who played as goalie on our hockey team would've raised his hand, but he was locked in as a defenseman. He used lacrosse to stay active and condition for hockey, not to practice being goalie. Seeing him just sit there and not volunteer, I started remembering the last hockey season—how I hated running out of breath and how I was already breathing way too hard after the lacrosse drills from five minutes before. Without thinking too hard about it, I put my hand in the air.

"I'll give it a shot," I said. It was kind of an impulsive decision, but that meant no running for me. *Sign me up*.

The only problem was that I had never played goalie before. But I was ready to learn. The lacrosse coaches were two players from Tufts University, a local college. For them, lacrosse was supposed to be fun. This was great because, in hockey, everyone played to such a high level. Especially if you played for a school team, you were expected to be dialed all the way in because, if you lost, everyone would be upset. But with lacrosse, the coaches didn't expect any of the players to be superstars or train like world-class athletes. Since it was more about learning the game, I didn't worry so much about being the best one on the field or making sure we won game after game. I could try to get better at my own pace and still have a good time while doing it.

I spent the rest of that first practice getting shots taken at me. Playing goalie was just a really hard game of catch—a game I wasn't the best at but also not the worst at either. I could hold my own at least. The only real issue (and one of the only things I took away from that practice) was that I would have to wear shin guards. When I played hockey, I'd wake up the next day sore, but playing lacrosse was a whole different level. Every day I went home, my legs would be *covered* in bruises, to the point where I said I'd never get back in the net without shin guards on again, even though (for whatever reason) lacrosse goalies weren't supposed to wear them. No one cared when I wore them, though, and even if they did, I put sweatpants on over the guards, so it's not like anyone could tell.

My first lacrosse season went by extremely fast. I had very minimal anxiety attacks, so I won't bore you by telling you about the whole season. But I will say that the closest I came to having an anxiety attack was when I forgot my cleats at home. Unlike hockey, the lacrosse gear never freaked me out or made me feel trapped. All I had to wear was one big chest pad, elbow pads, and my helmet (plus the shin guards, but those were optional). If I had to stop in the middle of a practice and go home, I only had to take off the helmet, and I'd be good. Likewise, the cleats never bothered me either. I only started to feel anxious when I realized that, because I left them, I wouldn't be able to play the game. But even when I started to panic, I figured that the awesome part about playing as goalie was that I didn't have to run; I just had to stand in front of the net. Crisis averted (and not even really a crisis, not when you compare it to my time playing hockey)—I played the whole game in my regular shoes!

Navigating lacrosse was way easier. My mom didn't have to come to the practices as much, especially with Nathan's family there. With lacrosse, my bond with Nathan and his family grew stronger. It wasn't like hockey where we were on different teams. It was all of us together. That's partially why I played lacrosse all through high school too. Actually, me, Chris, and Nathan started our high school's lacrosse team from the ground up. (This was the year that Nathan, who's a year younger than us, entered eighth grade and was able to play on the high school team.) When Justin played, he played for a nearby city league because our school didn't have one. But me, Chris, and Nathan wanted to play together as part of our school, so we went up to every kid who played hockey with us and said something along the lines of: "Hey, we know you like playing hockey, but when you want to train in the offseason, don't bother going to a weight room. Just join our lacrosse team instead."

We basically recruited every hockey player this way. As for a coach, one of the middle school teachers had played lacrosse in college, so he volunteered. From there, we built the whole team. My freshman year, we started as a club team; in sophomore year, we were JV; and by my junior year, we were varsity. And today, the team still exists.

Even back before high school, when I first started playing lacrosse, I thought the sport would be good for me, way better than hockey ever was. I still didn't fully believe all the adults who were talking to me about "progress" and "doing better." All I knew was that lacrosse was getting me through the last stretch before summer break, and I couldn't wait to finally be done with seventh grade forever. The school year seemed to last for an eternity, even though I had an insane amount of absences. I failed at least one quarter in every class and did the bare minimum to pass the rest of them. I just wanted it to be done and over.

I had never been happier for a semester to end in my life.

How Was Your Summer?

"How are you feeling about school?" my new therapist, Shelly, asked me while placing a board game piece down on the table. Therapy was different with her. When I talked about my problems and life with Jessie, it felt like an interrogation. I would sit in a chair and look at her while she sat at her desk across the room, writing what I said down on a clipboard and notepad. The only part missing was a "bad cop" and a single lightbulb hanging from the ceiling.

Sessions with Shelly worked better though. She sat on the same couch with me, so it felt more like a two-sided conversation, as if I were talking to a friend rather than someone my mom paid to try and understand my problems. The sessions didn't seem as serious, and instead of staring at me and trying to dissect my body language like I was some kind of science experiment, Shelly would pull out different board games to play. That day, we were playing Topple.

I didn't have to think hard before answering Shelly's question. At first, the thought of eighth grade terrified me. I imagined running to the car, running home, and the familiar pit in my stomach that would worsen when school started. But then I tried to think more positively. I was going to be in the same part of the school that I was in last year, so I would know the building. The best news was that my math teacher, the one who limited bathroom passes, was getting a different job and transferring.

With an open mind, I walked into school ready for my first day of eighth grade. My homeroom teacher was my science teacher, Mr. Miller, and after Ms. Summers, I would say he was the second-most supportive teacher to me. He was very passionate about making the kids learn from hands-on projects and wasn't the type to throw a packet at you and sit in his chair for the whole class. Instead, we'd either build cool projects like catapults in the woodworking room or go to the science lab and use the equipment there. When I was in his room, I had moments where I didn't even feel like I was at school. I don't know if you can tell at this point, but that was a pretty huge deal for me.

Mr. Miller was the same way about his homeroom class. In seventh grade, homeroom was used to make kids sit at their desks and catch up on work, or the teacher would give basic school announcements. But after taking attendance and making sure everyone who was supposed to be in school was there, he didn't care about forcing kids to sit in their seats or giving an early-morning lecture. This made me feel so much better. The previous year, I practically never went to homeroom, other than the rare occurrence when Zombie Matt strolled in, so this was a huge relief. I didn't have to worry about homeroom too much anymore. I just had to make sure I at least got there to say, "I'm here," before it ended.

Once I figured out homeroom, the rest of the first day was easy. Every teacher asked the same icebreaker: "How was your summer?"

"I went on a cruise."

"I got a puppy."

"I played video games."

The best part about those first-day conversations is that the teachers don't care who answers, so I didn't have to say a single thing all day until I went home. Well, except for in math class, where I had to tell my new teacher a fun fact about myself. My fun fact was, you guessed it, that I was a triplet—a fact that wasn't very fun for him because he'd heard it two other times that day from my brothers. But even though my new math teacher was strange and definitely just an awkward dude, he was way more lenient about bathroom passes. He was already a better replacement.

When I went home after school that day, a realization hit me: no more getting to see Nathan as often, considering he was at a different school, and no more free time and days at home. Now, I had to face the reality that I was back in school until summer again. Apart from the *last* week of school, the *first* week of school is the easiest. For the whole first week, all anybody has to worry about is getting used to their schedule, so no one is miserable yet. But after that first week, it sinks in for everyone that they'll all be here for a while, doing the same thing . . . every day.

My biggest fear was having a repeat of seventh grade, and I tried to find new loopholes around my anxiety attacks so I could manage them better. This is when I decided I wasn't going to make my mom bring me to school at all this year. I didn't even want to try it anymore. If I were going to have an anxiety attack and run home, I would leave my mom out of it. She had work to do at a different school, and I was done making her life more difficult to make the beginning of my day easier.

My brothers had always gone to school early to eat breakfast and hang out with their friends before class started. That's what I started to do too. Even though I tried this last year and failed, I knew my challenges and how to avoid them this year. I hated going into school on time with everyone else because there would be students everywhere, up and down the halls, and it would be loud and intimidating. I realized that by going to school early with my brothers, I could beat the crowd by getting in before them. That's when it started to work. I would go into school with my brothers about half an hour early, and we would all go to the cafeteria and eat cereal. Then, I would go to homeroom about three minutes before everyone, so I would already be in class instead of dealing with the kids stampeding through the halls.

This worked for a while and was only really an option in the mornings. Throughout the day, I still had my moments of hiding in the nurse's bathroom and standing in bathroom stalls. But for making it into the school building, getting there early helped me a lot. Most mornings, I would hang out with friends in the cafeteria, even though my brothers would do most of the talking, and as for the mornings when I wasn't in the socializing mood or was just feeling really down, I would grab my food from the cafeteria and eat in Ms. Summers's room.

My biggest problem wasn't getting into the building anymore. Not saying my anxiety totally vanished, but it was better, whether I wanted to believe it or not. Now, my toughest challenge was making it through the day and tolerating school.

The whole "social" part of the day exhausted me. I hated seeing people I kind of knew and having to fake happiness around them, making my life look picture-perfect, so I never held conversations for very long. I didn't feel like myself—ever. My anxiety and paranoia told me over and over that I wanted to be at home, and that was all I seemed to think about, the only thing going through my head all the time. I felt like I had no personality, which meant my anxiety *became* my personality. I started to believe that was the only interesting part of me.

When I talked to my mom and Ms. Summers about it, they both said that they understood how I was feeling, and I just needed to give it time. And that's what I did. I went to school and tried to branch out into different friend groups, but even when school ended and me and my brothers would go to our classmate Alex's house, the overthinking would continue.

We had been friends with Alex for years because of hockey, and he lived across the street from the school. (I mean, the school's parking lot was basically his front yard.) I knew I could run home if I had to, but even that thought didn't comfort me, since I was trying really hard not to run away and embarrass myself anymore. Hanging out with him, my brothers, and a bunch of other kids from the hockey team, I realized how much my anxious thoughts controlled my mind. I spent all my time at his house waiting to go home or thinking about how I had to do the same thing tomorrow. School days felt like they lasted for two months, not seven hours, and I never got a break from my thoughts. My life either consisted of having anxiety attacks or *thinking* about having anxiety attacks.

That's when my mom pitched the idea of therapy to me again. I was extremely hesitant, knowing what happened last time. The only thing worse than anxiety, depression, and paranoia was . . . nothing. I didn't want to be *nothing* again—no thoughts, just a body. Still, I was in a very difficult place in my head. While I hated the thought of seeing another therapist, I did need help. I agreed to try it again.

Sooner than later, I was walking in to meet Shelly. Just like last time, my mom came in with me for the first session. Shelly was made aware of my history with anxiety, as well as the medication I was on. Then, we all got to know each other by doing my least favorite part of therapy—answering ice breakers before I started venting about how horrible my life was going. Way worse than the ice breakers at school, where most of the time I didn't have to say a word.

Thankfully, when Shelly and I talked, it felt natural. There was more to focus on, like Topple, which let me be more open and get comfortable with her faster. I was not anywhere near ready to be open with Jessie, so I went into every session with a closed mind, annoyed that I had to be there at all. With Shelly, though, I walked in ready to rewire my brain, and the more I talked to her, the more I felt comfortable talking to other people. For the first time ever, therapy was going well.

Shelly had me book an appointment with her every weekend. I lived for these weekends. Not only because I didn't have to go to school and I could hang out with Nathan, but also because I really did enjoy therapy. More than that, I liked showing my mom that I was making progress, for real this time. With Shelly, I drew, played games, and started to understand . . . there's no reason for why I feel the way I feel.

Ever since I first started having anxiety, everyone has tried to find the root of the problem. As if, by finding where it originated, it would magically be solved and disappear. But Shelly didn't focus on the "why." She made me realize that there isn't always a bigger picture. There's a now. And the now controls your feelings and your life, not the past. If you are in a situation that makes you feel anxious, then you feel anxious, and you have to find something to do about it. I liked that way of looking at it. No longer was it someone's or something's *fault* that I had anxiety. Instead of trying to cast blame, I could just work on finding ways to better deal with it.

On the days when we didn't play board games, Shelly had me draw with her. This is when I found a skill that I still use today: characterizing my thoughts and feelings. Shelly told me to view each emotion as a different creature in my head—funny because that's exactly what Jessie tried to teach me when talking to me about *Inside Out*. This time, though, I was drawing out my emotions on paper.

The first time, Shelly told me to draw "a situation that makes me feel anxious." I drew myself outside a hockey rink with a little character next to me, representing my anxiety, who told me not to go inside. Shelly then explained to me that if I viewed these characters (or emotions) as separate from myself, they would be easier to control or get away from.

Finally, I saw an actual result from therapy. My anxious thoughts didn't go anywhere, but drawing them out changed how I looked at them. My emotions were no longer me, but a *part* of me.

Now I just had to figure out who I was without them.

What Are You Eating?

As time went on, I tried to practice the new strategies Shelly gave me, but it was difficult. In class, I would tell myself that it wasn't *me* thinking terrible thoughts; it was the characters in my brain. That didn't really work right away, since believing it was harder than thinking it.

The days went on, and my pills still weren't doing anything. I started to think I was either immune or the doctor gave me a placebo. But the adults in my life told me to keep taking them, so I did. I had no problem with staying on them. I mean, it's not like they were changing how my days went.

Sometimes, though, I purposefully didn't take the new pills. I wanted to see if I could feel a difference without them, and to no surprise, I felt exactly the same. How could the first pill I took, the little red one, make me forget half my day, but this one not affect me at all? I kept asking myself this question and became more worried. What if all the pills I'd taken before hit me all at once, and I went crazy?

Meanwhile, the pit in my stomach only grew worse. Eighth grade was the beginning of more intense stomach pain. When I first told my mom and Shelly about my stomach sometimes hurting, I explained how it would happen during anxiety attacks but then go away. This time, though, I wasn't feeling anxious, but my thoughts alone would cause the stomach pain—and way more pain than usual. My mom scheduled a doctor's appointment for me.

I had told my doctor about the day at baseball before, and he brought it up again during this appointment. "Yes, it's exactly like that," I told him.

He nodded, wrote something in his chart, and then instructed me to lie down on the examination table, where he pushed on my stomach and chest while asking me all kinds of questions, specifically about my physical, not mental, health.

"What are you eating?" he asked.

Truthfully, I wasn't eating well. I thought school lunch was nasty, so I only ate cereal in the morning. After school, I'd eat candy and drink soda, waiting way later to have dinner at night.

"Yep, that's it," he said. "You need to start eating better." He then asked me about the medication I was taking, and I told him it wasn't doing anything. He nodded and upped my dosage, saying I now had to take two pills a day instead of one.

He also said that I had to keep a food journal. Even though I knew my stomach pain was from my anxiety, not my diet. Me, Nick, and Chris were always eating the same things, and they weren't having stomach issues. To this day, even when we go out to eat, the waiter will put down three of the exact same dishes in front of us. Truthfully, I wasn't sure a food journal would help because I wasn't focused on anything in my life except my anxiety. I could have been eating the best meal of my life, but if you asked me about how it tasted, all I'd be able to tell you were my anxious thoughts while I was eating. That's kind of hard to explain to a doctor, though, so I didn't say anything.

Life continued, but now with a notepad to document what I ate and an extra 10-milligram pill of fluoxetine. I don't know why anyone thought a 13-year-old kid would take a food journal seriously, but I ate however I wanted and wrote down what I *thought* I ate at the end of the week, instead of meal by meal. With an extra 10 milligrams, I started to feel a little different—not like before when I was losing my memory, but a similar numb feeling with me constantly zoning out. Almost like my body was 100 times calmer, but my head wasn't. I was still thinking the same anxious thoughts; my body just didn't match.

I was about three months into the pill, four months into therapy, and halfway through the school year. I had the rest of the school year and summer to get my life together before high school, and I was getting nervous. One more quarter until all the students had to choose their high school classes, and I didn't want to think about it too much. Actually, I couldn't think about it, or I'd stress myself out for no reason.

High school was still so far away.

Or so I told myself.

Starting Over, Again?

Realizing I needed a different guidance counselor than Mrs. Casey and that Ms. Summers couldn't always be around since she had a whole other job to do, I started to see the other guidance counselor, Mrs. Farley—a very nice lady but, honestly, someone who didn't give me much to work with. Seeing Mrs. Farley never required an appointment, meaning it was up to me to visit her when I needed to. Except I wasn't the type to go out of my way to talk to someone, and that goes double for when I'm not fully comfortable with the person. Before, I had teachers setting up my meetings with Mrs. Casey. Now, I only saw Mrs. Farley if Ms. Summers or the school nurse convinced me to walk down to her office.

On the every-now-and-then occasion that I did meet with her, Mrs. Farley and I mostly talked about school issues while I talked to Shelly about more important life stuff. I brought up that I couldn't focus and how I frequently zoned out, but her only advice seemed to be: "Pay attention more." Not super helpful. Like, I *would* if I *could*.

That third quarter came around, and it was time to talk about high school classes. My future guidance counselor from high school came to my school to meet with my parents, Mrs. Farley, and me. They met without me first and then pulled me out of class for 10 minutes to join the end of the meeting. This is when I met Mr. Stephens for the first time, and on first impression, he seemed very friendly and nice, like he really was excited to get to know me next year. Mrs. Farley filled him in on everything we'd been talking about, and while it should have been Ms. Summers who explained because she definitely knew more, Mr. Stephens still got the gist of all I had to offer.

We talked about the classes I'd take in high school and agreed I would take all the basics. There were three levels: CPS (college prep with support), CP (college prep), and honors. I took all CPS classes, so I learned all the same material as CP kids, just with two teachers in my classes instead of one. I also told them I wanted to be a part of the CTE program, which stood for "Career and Technical Education," but all the students just called them "shops" or "trades." The last thing we talked about was foreign language. Since sixth grade, every time kids took their foreign language class, I took an extra help hour. They told me I wasn't going to take a foreign language in high school, and instead, they wanted me to take more extra help classes.

I had absolutely no urge to take a foreign language class, but I still felt so brainless. When we talked about it, they all tried to be nice, but I couldn't help but feel like everyone secretly thought I was a moron. Familiar thoughts went through my head: *How much of an idiot am I? I'm never going to get out of these extra help classes. I'm not unintelligent; this is just because of my anxiety.* I now know that, sure, I had some problems learning as a kid, but my anxiety did have a lot to do with why I did poorly in school. Coming to that realization took a lot of time, though, and as a student, talking about my grades, performance, or class placement stung.

The conversation ended, and I gave Mr. Stephens a handshake. We both said, "See you soon," and I went back to class. Except I was not excited to see him soon. That would mean I would be a freshman in high school, something I really didn't want to be.

I went to therapy that next weekend and talked to Shelly about it. She explained to me that when I moved into high school, I would be nervous, but that's normal.

"Every single freshman is gonna be nervous," she said. "It's a big switch. Lucky for you, you've made a big switch before when you went from sixth to seventh grade. That experience wasn't good, but at least now you know you can do it. And this time will be different."

This was one of the first times I didn't believe what Shelly said. As the cherry on top, after a couple more sessions, I got bad news: Shelly had gotten a better job opportunity somewhere else and was leaving.

I was mad. For the first time ever, therapy was working for me, but the second I thought something would finally change in my life, Shelly was up and leaving. I only got angrier over the fact that it was all about money. I understood that therapy was Shelly's job, but I still felt frustrated that she was going to get paid more to listen to someone else's problems. On top of that, with the end of eighth grade, the same thing happened with Ms. Summers. She would stay at her middle school job, but I would have to move to high school without her. I started to grow a hatred for all therapists and guidance counselors. Jessie, Shelly, Ms. Summers, Mrs. Farley, Mrs. Casey—I opened up to all of these people, only for them to be gone one day.

It crushed me. I made the decision that I wouldn't go to therapy again. I just didn't have it in me to share my story with someone new again, only to relive the baseball day all over.

Leaving therapy, I also quit fluoxetine. I didn't want to take it anymore. I was sick and tired of all the different medical solutions being thrown at me, and I could feel the pill start to take away more of me. My anxiety was me, and I couldn't figure out who I was without it. When the pills would take away my anxiety, even though that's what we all wanted, it felt like it was taking away my personality. I didn't feel human.

This is when I started to look to my family for more help. They already helped before, but at this point, I put all of my trust in them. My brothers, especially—because they were just like me, except without the anxiety. They were perfect examples of how I could be "normal" too.

FRESH

Christopher

Me and Nick had different interests growing up. Nick is very passionate, confident, and opinionated. But I'm the opposite—shy, easily impressed by everyone around me, and a homebody. He liked to go out and walk around with his friends. I liked being home or playing sports. Because Nick liked photography and had his own interests, he was in his own lane.

Still, we got along well. We understood that we didn't *have* to like the same things to have a lot of fun anyway. When we hung out with Nate or other friends, Nick would make me laugh the most, but because of our differences, I spent the whole summer after eighth grade studying Chris—music, clothes, how he would talk to people, everything. A lot of the time, Chris was copying our older brother, Justin, but Chris would put his own spin on things. Chris was my cool little brother (even though he was only born two minutes after me), and nothing ever bothered him. He could just go with the flow and chill, something I was trying to replicate for myself. It was like trying to illegally download his happiness into my own brain.

Those two months after eighth grade put a timer on my personality. Not that I had to *change* my personality or anything. The way I saw it, I had to *find* a personality. Because I didn't have one yet. I didn't feel like a human being with purpose, having fun and enjoying life. I felt like an empty shell without any real interests or passions. No dreams to chase or anything unique to do. There was no goal other than going home and going to bed. Somehow, I had to build confidence and learn who I was before I started freshman year. The only way to do this was to follow Chris's lead. He seemed to have it figured out.

All that summer, I was Chris's shadow. When we went to the mall to buy clothes for the school year, he would pick out a shirt, and I'd grab the same one in a different color. When he bought clothes from Lyrical Lemonade, a music video production channel on YouTube, I would too. It gave me "permission" to also like the shirts, almost like I needed somebody else to sign off on the clothes I wore. Even with music, I would bob my head while he sang Wiz Khalifa's verse on "Payphone" by Maroon Five. He also got me to listen to the popular rappers at the time: Lil Uzi Vert, Travis Scott, Migos, Lil Skies. Chris would do the hard work of discovering new artists and clothes, and then he would see me enjoying the same things as him. Inevitably, he'd say, "You're copying me. Stop copying me." But for me, it bypassed my anxiety. I could do that because I'd seen somebody who's like me doing it. It was like there was already an example or variation of who I could be out there.

I was just tagging along to everything that Chris did, but seeing him enjoy things made me enjoy them even more. If *he* was having fun playing hockey, I knew *I* would have fun playing hockey. I never followed Nick because I just wasn't passionate about the hobbies he had, like photography, for instance. But once I saw Chris try something, I felt comfortable trying it as well. That's when I knew I could do it too.

The cool thing about Chris was that I think he understood my need to try and fit in and be like him. Yeah, he'd tell me to stop every now and then, but he never *really* got mad at me for copying him. Actually, he was a huge help with my anxiety. Whenever I had a panic attack in public, he would walk me to the bathroom to take a breather and wait outside until I calmed down. Or if it was really bad, he would stand in the stall next to me and talk me out of it. He had a way of making even the worst moments feel survivable.

He'd say, "We're just going to grab a few things and go home," or, "There aren't that many people around—nobody's going to see you." The most helpful, but also the most simple, was when he'd tell me to just breathe. Together, we'd inhale and exhale to stop my hyperventilating.

Chris helped me with everything, well into freshman and sophomore year and beyond. He'd even work with me through harder hockey practices and the anxiety of wearing a tight, button-up dress shirt to school on game days. Because of him, I saw my first glimpse of what a life focused on the things you love is—a life without anxiety.

You Think That's Hard?

My first introduction to high school was through, like most things, Justin.

School was not Justin's cup of tea. He stayed up late playing video games and online poker, which made him sleep in so late that he had a ton of absences. I remember once, as an elementary-school kid, I barged into his room and sat on the bed. Justin had a "one triplet in my room at a time" policy when we were younger, so I got lucky that no one else was in there with him. Figuring that since he was in high school and could help me out, I showed him my homework: a worksheet with multiplication tables. I complained about how difficult it was, how I just didn't *get* math.

"You think that's hard?" Justin said, turning around in his computer chair and grabbing his backpack. "Look at this."

He pulled out a thin folder, pulled out an assignment, and slapped it down in front of me. It was his algebra homework. My mouth fell open. The problems had *letters* in them. What sick, screwed-up individual thought of that?

That's when the dread of high school first set in. *I'm never going to be able to do that*, I thought. *No way.*

Elementary-school Matt was right. I don't know if I would have been able to do high school without Nick and Chris there to support me.

The high school wasn't within walking distance, not like our other two schools were. The walk there would take about 17 minutes, so my mom drove me and my brothers on our first day. Dropped off at the front of the school, it set in how big of a test this would be for me. I would be entering a building without Ms. Summers or classes with my brothers. I wouldn't know the building layout anymore, and I would have a harder time escaping to run home if I had to. I felt just like I did when I switched to seventh grade—knots in my stomach, like I was about to throw up. My thoughts immediately went to four years in the future, when I'd be sprinting back to the car with a diploma in my hand.

My first class of the day was "study skills," a.k.a. my "stupid class." The class had three teachers and seven students from different grades. As a freshman, the two seniors were intimidating, but at least one was my friend's older brother. Plus, it was easy to mind your business in study skills, especially because the seniors didn't care at all. About anything.

I didn't find out what study skills was all about on my first day though. Instead, I sat down at my desk, shot up my hand, and asked to use the bathroom. I didn't have to go; I just had to figure out where the bathroom *was*. My goal was to memorize the building as much as I could on my first day. The teacher stopped explaining how the class worked and wrote me a pass.

The bathroom closest to study skills was in the basement, next to the cafeteria. After finding it, I didn't go back to my classroom. Instead, I walked up to the first floor and found the nurse's office, where I stopped to check on the bathroom situation there. The only thing I accomplished in the rest of my classes was finding the bathrooms and learning the school building. I asked to go to the bathroom in every class but then used the time to measure the distance from there to the nurse's office or walk from class to class, memorizing my schedule. When school ended, I didn't know a thing about what my classes would be like or who my teachers were. For me, the most important part of school was never the classes; it was how I would escape them if I had to.

Once school ended, I went outside and stood with all my friends and brothers. We talked about our school day. Then we went home. I wasn't ready to do that every day for the rest of the school year. No—for an entire *four years*.

Yet another curveball: A month into high school, my mom stopped driving us, and we took the public bus instead. Riding the Massachusetts Bay Transit Authority was unhinged, packed with a mix of adults on their way to work and other students getting to school. You learned to just mind your business and keep your head down. One time on our way back from school, a kid had ripped out a metal "No Parking" sign from the ground and brought it on the bus. When he got off, he just left the sign in his seat.

Nick was in charge of the whole bus thing since he had an app on his phone that would tell us when to walk to the bus stop. I would get ready for school and wait on the couch, and he would tell me when to go. This helped a lot because the anticipation of looking at the bus getting closer and closer on the app would've sent me into a frenzy.

We still went to school early like we did in eighth grade, but this time, all the kids would wait outside and talk in front of the entrance. Nick and Chris were the only reasons I knew lots of people. Groups in high school don't blend, but I still had a mix of friends. I knew people from kindergarten through sixth grade, from seventh and eighth grade, and from sports—but I wasn't able to make more friends outside of these groups by myself.

Thankfully, the cool part about being a triplet was the association with my much more social brothers. Nick was friends with girls who would also talk to me because they were cool with him. Same with Chris. He had friends from his music classes and upperclassmen he befriended. Even though I would never be the type to start a friendship, Nick and Chris made it easy. Sure, I had

Nathan, but I only saw him outside of school because he was in eighth grade. So, Nick and Chris made all of my friends for me while I focused on figuring out myself. Because of my brothers, I had at least one friend to talk to in every class. And while these friends and I wouldn't hang out outside of school, at least I never felt like I was looked at for my anxiety anymore.

Also, being a triplet made us so-called "popular" because it was interesting to people. It's not like people wanted to be our friends *because* we were triplets, but they knew who we were before ever meeting us—we were the local triplets. My mom working at one of the public schools in the city made us pretty popular too because people would know us through her. So many people would tell me that my mom was awesome and nice to them when they were at her school.

My favorite part of school, other than its ending, was the last class of the day. It was "exploratory." Exploratory included different "shops" like carpentry and electrical and other vocational training. In order to pick a shop, the first school year was basically a trial of all of them. Two weeks of each. For the electrical vocation, you practiced splicing wires together. In cosmetology, you practiced cutting a mannequin's hair. And in carpentry, you made cutting boards. (My mom still has the cutting board we made.) My older brother, Justin, had taken the carpentry class when he was in high school, so me and Chris already knew we wanted to do carpentry. But the exploratory was so fun because every two weeks, I could try a different hands-on program.

The differences between those classes and my others were huge. When I was in culinary school for a week, I was focused and happy because, for an hour of the school day, I only had to make cookies. But when I was in health class, I was so bored. It was my third class of the day, so I always fell asleep in it. Anxious thoughts and late-night video games ruined my sleep cycle, so I usually crashed in study skills or health, the classes that were least important to me. The sleeping wasn't even something I tried to do. I would just put my head on my desk, trying to escape the anxious pit in my stomach or crazy out-of-nowhere thoughts, and pass out.

Was all of high school going to be like this?

Do You Know Charlie?

In high school, I never asked for help. All of my classes had two teachers, and they would check if I needed anything. I would say no, even in study skills where "extra help" was the whole point of the class. It was only when a teacher saw that I was doing the work wrong that they would step in. But it was up to them to start helping. I was embarrassed to have the teacher standing next to my desk, teaching me the same material all over again while other students were in the room. I felt exactly the way I did when I started middle school, except this time, I didn't have Ms. Summers.

I missed Ms. Summers a lot. Of the two teachers in every class, one would be the main teacher who gave the lesson, and the other would walk around to help students. The second teacher was typically an exhausted, miserable college student in training who hated their job. None of them were as comforting or patient as Ms. Summers. The closest person I had to her was my guidance counselor, Mr. Stephens.

I hated the first couple of meetings with Mr. Stephens. With the way all of my other therapy or guidance counselor sessions went, I didn't want to explain my story to him because, in four years when I graduated, it wouldn't matter to him anymore. Thankfully, my mom, dad, and middle school counselor had already met with him and explained my backstory, so he at least knew the gist. I only started feeling comfortable around him after meeting with him several times. Even then, we only met once every two weeks, and I needed more help than that.

I don't know whose idea it was, but one day, when I walked into Mr. Stephens's office, there was another student there with him. Thinking I walked in on a meeting, I shut the door and waited outside. Except, Mr. Stephens opened the door back up and told me I could come in. I was confused but walked in anyway, taking a seat across from him.

"Do you know Charlie?" Mr. Stephens asked. He nodded to the other kid sitting next to me.

"Yeah," I said. Charlie was in my history class. I never really talked to him since he had his friend group, and I had mine. Actually, we didn't have a single mutual friend in common. The only real similarity we shared was carpentry: We'd both signed up for it, so now we would see each other in every carpentry class until we graduated.

Mr. Stephens then proceeded to explain that Charlie and I would start meeting with him at the same time. Not only did I think this was the dumbest idea ever, but I was angry. Mr. Stephens was the only person I had left, outside of my family, who I could talk with one-on-one, but he took that away. I had no idea why—maybe he only had one time slot to meet with us—but I never asked. All I knew was that Charlie did *not* care about my problems and *definitely* didn't want to hear me talk about them.

For the rest of the counseling session, Charlie and I played games to get to know each other better. I was not excited to go back to counseling again because, next time, we would actually bring up all the stuff I didn't want anyone else to know, let alone some kid I just met. And to make matters worse, he was in every single one of my vocational exploratories: culinary, cosmetology, electrical, and then carpentry. We would always be seeing each other, just never speaking.

That being said, my freshman year had gone better than I thought it would, even if I still wasn't where I wanted to be: My whole personality was a loose version of Chris's but with anxiety mixed into it. My sophomore year went about the same, though it was a year full of even more challenges and tests. Still plenty of personality finding and anxiety, but this time, Nathan was there. Plus, me and Chris started the day in history class and ended it together in carpentry, so he pep-talked me through all the rough mornings and anxious afternoons.

All sophomore year, I would talk to Mr. Stephens a lot. But so would Charlie. At the same time. It got to the point where Charlie knew essentially everything about me: how I studied buildings, spent way too much time mapping out escape plans, and even figured out how to go to the bathroom without running into 20 kids sharing JUULs and dab pens. Charlie knew everything you've read about me so far. Actually, Charlie knew even more than that.

It's a two-way street though. I know that Charlie didn't have a father figure at home. He grew up in the projects, hated public speaking, and didn't feel comfortable during long car rides. I also know way more, but I'll keep those secrets safe. I'm not going to be the one to break our unspoken pact.

The second we left Mr. Stephens's office, we didn't say a word to each other. I saw him every day in class, but we hardly talked. Instead, we would sometimes make eye contact and nod. Just an implied respect for privacy.

The last time I saw Charlie was at our graduation, but I think about the whole ordeal pretty often. I hope he's doing better. I don't think we were ever going to be friends because of how much we were forced to know about each other, but a mutual respect did form. On the rare occasion we did speak, either outside of school or in carpentry, we only murmured a few words to check in with each other, asking, "You good?" We'd respond with a yes, but who knows if that was true.

Even still, I hope he knows how much I appreciate him keeping my secrets to this day.

What's the First Thing You'd Grab?

Mid-2019, about to start my sophomore year, I felt the most confident I'd ever been. That summer, I broke out of my box more than I did the previous year, spending more time at the pool and at the cape with Nathan's family than inside playing Fortnite (although I did end up playing way too much of that too). I took a trip to Las Vegas, where Justin was living for the summer and playing in professional poker tournaments, and pushed myself out of my comfort zone by being far away from home in what I thought would be an "adventurous" vacation (but not really since there's not a lot to do in Vegas when you're under 21). I looked forward to taking my driver's test, with my 16th birthday being right around the corner. Basically, everything was coming up. Well, until my family experienced one of the worst things a family can experience.

On August 9, 2019, our house caught on fire.

My childhood home was split into three floors. My family took the top two floors, and my aunt and uncle lived in the bottom "apartment." Even though we essentially lived in the same house, I wasn't close to them, mostly because of past family problems and situations. Yeah, I would see them on special occasions like Christmas Eve or rare family reunions, but other than that, the only time I saw my aunt was when I went outside to play basketball. She's a pack-a-day type of person, and cigarettes are like a sixth finger to her. She'd always be outside on the deck smoking, except during cold winters with lots of snow when she would smoke inside, and it would come up through the vents and make our whole living room smell. I couldn't tell you how many times one of my relatives would say something like, "She better be careful to put those out, or she'll burn the whole house down."

One day, it happened.

Just like any other day, my aunt was using her old, plastic Home Depot bucket for an ashtray—the same one she'd probably been using for two decades. She flicked a still-lit cigarette into the bucket as usual but then stared as it burned a hole through the plastic. The cigarette butt fell through the hole, out of the bucket, and between the wooden planks that made her back deck. Under the deck was where we raked leaves during the fall season, so there were bags of twigs, grass, and other yard trash. Essentially, kindling.

My aunt watched as the fire very quickly started to spread—way faster than you might expect. She didn't think to call 911 for a firetruck or even tell anyone. Instead, she just went back inside and crawled into bed.

It wasn't long before the whole backside of the house was engulfed in flames. The fire started from under the back deck and crawled up the side of the house. Thankfully, my aunt had closed the door on her way inside. If she hadn't, the fire would have entered the home instead of traveling up the side. The whole first floor would have burned, which meant the second and third floors could have lost their foundation and collapsed. It's also possible that me, Justin, Chris, and my mom would not have had enough time to escape had that happened.

Once the flames grew high enough, a neighbor saw them, ran over to tell us, but then couldn't kick down our very heavy front door. She looked around, and there happened to be a police officer on our street, who was coincidentally handling an issue with a stolen car. The cop abandoned the stolen car problem and banged against our door with her foot, also trying to kick it down but failing. My mom, thinking it was Nick because he had left to go to a friend's house that morning, opened the door, confused. That's when the cop on the other side told her to get everyone out of the house immediately.

The fire happened in 2019, the year Fortnite was the most popular video game in the world. Since it was summertime, me, Justin, and Chris had been up until six in the morning playing the new competitive mode they'd just added, so when the fire broke out at two in the afternoon, we were all still asleep. I just remember my mom running into our room and yelling for me and Chris to wake up, telling us to leave the house. Since Justin's room was on the second floor, she had already stopped, woken him up, and grabbed our dog, a puggle named Trevor.

When people talk about house fires, they always ask, "If your house were burning down, what's the first thing you'd grab?" I can tell you from experience that when you're in that situation, the thought doesn't even cross your mind. The only thing that matters is getting out of the house as fast as you can. When my mom woke us up, me and Chris just looked at each other and started running. Chris actually jumped over our mom while going down the stairs. Like literally hurdled over her. *While* she was holding the dog.

Me and Chris stood outside the house and watched the fire. We realized that in our panic, we hadn't grabbed anything. We hadn't even grabbed pants. We were sitting on the curb in our boxers.

I guess the answer to that "What would you grab?" question differs from person to person. My mom loves our dog, so of course, she walked out with Trevor, who didn't have his leash or anything. She held him the entire time we waited for the firemen. Meanwhile, the cop walked out with my uncle and my aunt, who had grabbed a pack of cigarettes and some money so she could walk to the convenience store and buy more. Finally, Justin came out in a full color-coordinated outfit, a backward hat, a phone charger, all of his essentials, and a backpack filled with money. That backpack had all his winnings from his last poker tournaments in it. Five minutes after stepping outside, a friend came to pick him up, and Justin was out of there.

It took way longer than I anticipated for me and Chris to put clothes on. We had to have sat on that curb in our underwear for close to 20 minutes before a neighbor came up and offered us some track pants and workout shirts. The only problem was that our neighbor was taller than six feet, and at the time, I hadn't hit 5′5″. Me and Chris were swimming in his XXL clothes. I probably could've fit two extra legs in one of the pant legs, so if I wanted to walk anywhere, I had to hold the pants up myself.

Eventually, firemen came and started putting out the fire. That's when word started getting around the city, and friends came by to check on us. Since we lived in such a small neighborhood, everyone we knew was there: friends from school, teammates from hockey, their parents, neighbors. News anchors came, and so did people from the Red Cross, asking us if we needed a hotel. What people don't tell you, though, is that when your house catches on fire, contractors and insurance agents show up too. They swarmed my mom with business cards, trying to offer her the best deals and make a quick buck while actively watching my childhood home burn.

Since my dad worked at our school, he was an eight-minute walk away, so he immediately ran over as soon as he heard. Because me and Chris didn't grab anything when we evacuated, I took my dad's phone to call Nick and tell him what happened.

Nick was outside at a friend's, and since our friend lives at the very top of a hill in our neighborhood, Nick was watching as helicopters flew overhead in the general direction of our house. Even though he couldn't see the fire from that distance, he had a feeling something was wrong. But it still took three tries to get him to pick up the phone because he was swimming around in the pool. Nick still jokes that when he finally answered, I said, "Hey, not a big deal, but the house is burning down."

That's not exactly what I said. I just led with the whole "not a big deal" thing because I didn't want him to think someone was burned alive. Nick's dramatic, and I had to let him down easy.

"You can keep swimming, but I'm just telling you that when you come home, we're not sleeping here tonight," I told him. Nick was obviously upset, but he ended up staying out with his friends, considering there was no home to come back to.

By that point, the fire was finally out. The firefighters told us that we could go back inside, look around, and grab anything that wasn't damaged. Until then, it hadn't sunk in that my house would be taken away from me for a while. But walking around in the ashes and seeing all the wreckage, it hit me. My house, the one place in the world where I felt safe and comfortable, was gone.

We all walked through the house and cried, memories of our now-destroyed house flashing through our heads. I went into my room and grabbed my phone, which had been stepped on by firefighters while they were breaking the windows open. I changed out of my neighbor's old, baggy tracksuit and put on my clothes that smelled smoky. I put on shoes and socks, but my feet were wet from the water. I went over to our game room and looked through the doorway with a blank face. Everything was gone.

Me, Nick, and Chris shared two bedrooms on the third floor. (Remember, at one point, Chris took one bedroom for himself because he thought he was some kind of cool kid who needed his own room for some reason. But after a month, he gave up on that, and us three decided to share the two rooms instead.) One room had all three of our beds, and the other one had our computers, PlayStations, and games. Because the game room was at the back of the house, the fire was able to climb up and inside the two windows, burning up nearly everything. All of our belongings in that room—of course, some of the most expensive things in the house—were destroyed by flames or water damage, or broken because a firefighter had to throw them across the room to get to the fire.

It's extremely hard to think positively in a situation like that. I grew a hatred toward my aunt and uncle, and my emotions became more and more difficult to understand. I wasn't worried about where my aunt and uncle would end up. My aunt walking to the store to buy another pack of cigarettes while the firefighters were still putting out the fire felt like a punch in the face. What hurt even more was that my uncle and aunt's apartment was fine. The fire went up, not down, so they got to grab so much more. I'm grateful that my mom's photo albums and our baby pictures were at least safe. She's kept updated scrapbooks and journals since way before me, Nick, and Chris were born. Maybe even before Justin was born.

The only thing that survived in the game room was Nathan's birthday present: a hockey jersey. A few days before, the jersey was sitting on the couch, and since Nathan was coming over, Chris shoved it under a cushion, not knowing where else to hide it. We forgot about the jersey afterward, so it was still there when the fire broke out and when the firefighters flipped over the couch to save it from the flames, also saving the jersey in the process. Later, when me, Nick, and Chris turned the couch back over, we found the jersey wedged in the same place we left it, smelling terrible but still in mint condition.

The same day of the fire, we grabbed the jersey and drove to Nathan's birthday party. Beforehand, we went to the dry cleaner to drop off our clothes and then to our friend Alex's house. If you remember, Alex lived right across the street from our middle school. While we were all sitting on our front lawn during the fire, his mom came over and told us they were going to Plymouth for the week. If we wanted, we could use their house while they were away. My mom tried telling her that they didn't have to do that for us, but Alex's mom insisted. She handed her the key to their house.

Post-fire, me and my brothers sat in a total state of shock at Alex's house, silently staring at the wall as reality set in: We wouldn't be going home that night.

When Nathan texted us, saying there was still time to swing by his party and grab some cake, my mom pushed us out the door. There was no point in sitting around and being depressed at Alex's when we could be celebrating with Nate.

You might think that by walking into a party right after our house burned down, we would've killed the vibe. But by the time we got to Nathan's, everyone was already "partied" out. One of Nathan's million cousins had hit another cousin in the head with a hockey stick and put him in the ER earlier that day, so the Sturniolo disaster wasn't the issue on everyone's mind, especially because we all thought it wouldn't be long before we were back in our house again. No one really talked about the fire. We just ate cake, hung out, and then went back to Alex's that night to sleep.

My family spent a week at Alex's house. When they came back from vacation, though, they obviously needed their home back, so they gave us the keys to Alex's dad's apartment, who wasn't using it because he was deployed in Afghanistan. We stayed at his place while my parents went apartment hunting in the city. But as much as I am grateful to Alex's family for giving us as much as we needed, I wanted my house back. That apartment wasn't my home. I hated that everywhere I was living was temporary. And because my mom and dad could see how emotionally drained we were, they let me and my brothers do whatever we needed to cope. We ended up spending the rest of that summer staying at Nathan's instead of the apartment, playing video games and having pizza nights. Nathan's parents were doing everything to distract us from the fact that our house wasn't there anymore. His house basically turned into ours, and I felt like I had a home again.

By the time school started up, my family had found an apartment on the other side of the city near the high school. To say it was a small apartment for all six of us would be an understatement. Walking in, my mom and dad had their own bedroom on the right. After the fire, Justin had been living at a friend's house for a while, but when we signed the lease for the new apartment, he moved in and took the second bedroom. Since there were no other bedrooms, Nick claimed a tiny office space, and me and Chris put our new mattresses in the dining room for ourselves.

We had to throw away most of our furniture and clothes because of the smoke smell. The clothes that we *did* want to keep had to be dry-cleaned about 10 times to wash the scent out, so for the first little while, we only had about three or four outfits to rotate between every week. A lot of people in the city saw what we were going through and donated a bunch of different things that we needed. Someone gave us an old dining room table, and another gave us a couch from their man cave. We even had a small fundraiser event at a local tavern in town (what Chris called "a baby shower but for house fires"), and so many people and friends from the city came to support us. The only necessities we had to buy were beds and bed frames. Just about everything else came from people in the community.

I was very grateful . . . but also crushed. I felt bad that I was still so confused with my emotions after all the support, but it was truly the most up-and-down my life could be. I was having amazing moments sleeping at friends' houses and spending time at the pool, but then going back to a "temporary home" took away all my happiness. I hated having to start over with clothes and all of my belongings, and having to sleep on a mattress on the floor of a dining room.

The only thought keeping me going was that we just had to endure this for a couple of months. But here's something else no one tells you about house fires: Firefighters will try to calm you down by greatly underestimating how much time repairs will take. I guess no one wants to be the guy to tell you, "Oh, your house? Yeah, it's *cooked*." I can only assume that's why, back when me and Chris were sitting outside in our underwear and still watching the flames fizzle out from the curb, one firefighter said, "You might be able to go back in tonight."

My family all looked at each other, thinking, *Okay, that's probably not true*.

Sure enough, another firefighter came out and said, "It's looking more like two weeks now." Then another one said a month. And by the time they finished putting out the fire, we were told three months. From there, everyone just kept telling us a higher and higher number.

I have to cut them some slack, though. No one knew that, since this was August 2019, the world was about to experience a catastrophe unlike anything anybody had ever seen in their lifetimes: a pandemic that would shut everything down, make construction work impossible, and turn our three-month project into a *two-year* fever dream.

MASSACHUSETTS
DRIVER'S LICENSE
• BIRTHDATE •
08/01/03
• EXPIRES •
08/01/30
ID:19641996

Right on Red?

How many feet away can you park near a building that's on fire?

A) 300

B) 500

C) 1,200

D) 800

I looked at the screen and smiled. What a fitting question for where I was at in my life.

Once we settled into our new apartment enough, I had my mom bring me to the DMV to take my permit test. Unlike Nick and Chris, who didn't want to take away time from hanging out with friends, I wanted to learn how to drive more than anything. (As of 2025, Nick still hasn't gotten his driver's license—and I have questioned this every single day of my life since. It's been five years of driving my brothers around. I literally spend so much time pressing a gas pedal, I got tendinitis in my ankle. Do you know who usually gets tendinitis? People in their 40s and 50s, not 20-somethings. Like, this is outrageous.)

My study skills teacher that year was a very laid-back college student who didn't care what we were working on as long as we were being productive. Because of her, I spent weeks of school taking practice permit tests in that class. I didn't want to fail. I needed to get it.

Driving seemed fun, but above all else, I wanted a license because being able to leave situations whenever I wanted would change my life. That's the reason I had separation anxiety from my parents. Yes, they gave me comfort, but they were also my ticket out of places I didn't want to be. But now that I was 16, I could be my own escape.

I went to the DMV and waited for what seemed like an eternity, and eventually, they called my number to go take my permit test. Even though I was nervous, I was ready—I had been practicing for weeks.

"Alright, go to computer number two. If you get 18 out of 25 or higher, come back up to me. If you get any lower and fail, leave and come back in two weeks to take it again," the lady said to me before I went in.

I knew I could get 18 out of 25 questions right. I was doing good, getting a few wrong, but I was close. But suddenly getting nervous and starting to struggle, I then answered two more wrong, and I was down to my last question with a score of 17 out of 24. I had to answer this one correctly if I wanted to pass.

That's when the test gave me the "How many feet away can you park near a building that's on fire?" question.

With no hesitation, I clicked "C) 1,200."

The words "You failed" popped up on the screen. My heart fell into my stomach. The correct answer was "D) 800."

I was devastated and angry. Why would someone *not* want to park as far away as possible from a building on fire? I felt like the DMV was making fun of me and my house.

I walked out of the room and straight to my mom: "Looks like we're coming back in two weeks."

She was upset. She knew how badly I wanted this, but she was ready to bring me back in two weeks if that's what it took. I spent that time on practice tests—taking them in study skills, on my phone under the desk in other classes, and at home. I was not ready to fail again. The second I was able to, my mom took me back to the DMV, and I walked into the room, certain that I'd crush it.

I absolutely killed it with an 18 out of 24 score. I was the happiest I'd been in so long.

By the way, learning to drive in Massachusetts was wild. First of all, Boston is famous for road rage—people beeping their horns, swearing at nothing, and rolling down their windows to yell. Sometimes, people will spit on cars. I've even seen people jump out of their vehicles and threaten to beat somebody up. Even in less populated areas, people ride their bikes everywhere, so drivers start freaking out when bikers are riding in the middle of the road and causing traffic, going 25 miles per hour with a baby strapped to their back. That's why my mom and I thought it'd be best for me to start out in a parking lot.

My number-one goal was driving. If I wasn't out with our friend group or at school, I was practicing driving with my mom. And yeah, I had finally made enough progress that I was part of a friend group, one that was basically inseparable. Some of our closest friends were three girls who lived very close to Nathan. They were friends with Nick first, but then we all started to hang out at Nate's house together. And if we weren't at Nathan's house, we would all go to shopping centers or movie theaters. While I still had anxiety attacks, the cycle of hanging out with friends, working at the local grocery store, and driving with my mom was the most productive I'd ever been.

Driving school skyrocketed my confidence. I would go to one class a week, do textbook work, and watch videos. Paul, the driving instructor, would go over the videos with the class on the weekends. Other times, he'd pick me up from my house, and I would drive with him for an hour. Then, we'd pick up another student at their house, and they would drive me home so I could get observation hours. If a year earlier, you told anyone in my family that I would be driving around with strangers and making new friends, no one would've believed it.

Paul told me that I was one of the best students he'd had. The only time he ever told me I did something wrong was when I stopped the car for a bunny in the road. Even though he was happy I was paying attention, he explained that swerving or braking for an animal is the number one way to get rear-ended, so I shouldn't do it again. We both laughed and kept the lesson going.

In September, I finally finished driving school and had plans to take my driver's test on the ninth. I was so excited—very nervous, but mostly excited. When the day of my test came, I made sure to wake up as early as I could. The test was three cities over, and I hadn't driven there at all. But I was ready.

My mom let me drive to the test to warm up. I think we got there an hour before we were supposed to. There were no signs or anything that showed where the test would be, but we saw a cop in the parking lot. My mom got out of the car and went to talk to him about the test. Every time she talked to people in public, I would get nervous because I didn't want the conversation to be directed at me. My mom asked him if we were in the right spot for the driver's test, and he pointed across the street and said, "Yup, it starts right there."

He looked at me and waved me over to his car as well. He then asked me if I was the one taking the test.

"Yes," I said.

"I've seen people take the test thousands of times. You're gonna go two blocks, parallel park on the second, and then drive back over that way." He pointed at a side road in the distance. "If you stop at the red light, the instructor will tell you to take a right on red. But really, there's a sign that tells you not to. Don't fall for the trick."

I thanked him, he wished me luck, and my mom and I waited in our car for more people to show up. I saw the driving instructor and a couple of kids, so I walked over and hopped in line. A friend from baseball was there with his parents, so we waited in line together, not talking much because of nerves. When it was my turn, I jumped in the car and put on my seatbelt right away. I was as confident as I could be. I followed directions and drove like I would in my lessons.

Just like the cop said, the instructor tried to tell me to take a right on red, but I avoided the scam. I'm really lucky my mom decided to talk to the cop and get that advice because ordinarily, if the instructor told me to do anything, I would've done it without hesitation. The instructor could have told me to fly the car, and I would have found a way to make it happen. But because I avoided the right-on-red scam (and as I found out later, a lot of kids fell for it), I pulled back into the lot we started in and got the sign-off for my license.

Words can't describe how much that moment meant to me.

Nicolas

While I worked toward getting my license so I could drive all of us around, Nick and Chris spent that time with friends. Especially Nick. Being way more outgoing than me, he had a lot of friends outside of Nathan, and while I did hang out with him and his friends, he also liked to do stuff with them on his own too. Me and Chris would go to Nathan's house as usual, but Nick started to spend the night with other people and do his own thing.

One thing we always did as a group, though, was go to school sports games. One friend played volleyball, so we would go watch her. A lot of people showed up at those games: friends, boyfriends, siblings, and parents of the players. If I weren't friends with someone there already, then my friends were. So, I kind of knew everyone.

One night, I went to a game with my brothers and the two girls in our group to cheer on our friend. A girl I liked, who I'll refer to as Nancy, was there, so I spent most of the game trying to get to know her better. Meanwhile, Nick was chatting with some of our other friends, away from the rest of us.

After the game wrapped up, we walked one of Nick's friends, who we'll call Sarah, home since she lived nearby. He had been talking to her at the game all night, and while we headed to our own home, Nick explained to me that Sarah had a crush on me. Nick had a very slight idea that I was already talking to Nancy, but because of where I was at mentally, I never pursued my crushes. Me and Nick continued all the way home arguing about me dating Sarah.

"I think I want to try things out with Nancy. I really like her," I told him.

“Why don’t you just talk to Sarah? She’s cool, and you already know she likes you!”

From then on, the rest of our walk home was either filled with fighting, awkward silence, or Chris trying to break up the weird tension. This was typical, though. At this point in our lives, me and Nick were very short-tempered with each other. I love Nick, and I care about Nick, but the number of arguments we had about anything and everything felt pointless. Sometimes, our fights got so bad that we could barely stand to look at each other, but obviously, early apartment life made that impossible. In the confines of those small rooms, every argument we had was on full display for the family. And they happened a lot.

But that day after the volleyball game, I felt more confused than angry: Why did Nick care so much about who I wanted to date?

When we got home, Justin and my dad were out, and my mom wasn’t there either since she was probably working late. With the three of us in the apartment, me and Chris sat at our new desks in the dining room/our bedroom. I called Nathan to tell him about my day and what he missed at the volleyball game. And *again*, Nick brought up Sarah. (Nate was still on the phone, but he’s like a brother to us. He’s seen us argue countless times, so he’s used to the fights. His response is always funny, though. He just lets us yell and doesn’t voice his opinions unless we ask, or until hours have passed, when we’ve calmed down and the fight is already over.)

Before Nick could even finish his thought about Sarah, I stood up from my seat and screamed, “IF YOU LIKE HER SO MUCH, WHY DON’T *YOU* DATE HER?”

That’s when Nick screamed back at me, “I CAN’T BECAUSE I’M *GAY*!”

I sat back down in my seat.

Time froze. I was immediately in tears, and so was he. I couldn't help but instantly think about how difficult this was for him.

For my whole life, I wanted to be just like Nick. Yes, I followed Justin and Chris's hobbies, but that's because they were my favorite things too. But when I looked at Nick, I only ever saw confidence and strength. I was envious of the fact that he could go out with his friends in the big city of Boston without a single nervous bone in his body. He seemed to have everything all figured out. And all I ever wanted was to "have it all figured out," just like him. Our constant arguments stemmed from that jealousy.

Deep down, I knew this—I just didn't want to admit it. What I didn't know, though, was that on the night of the volleyball game, Nick felt jealous too. Jealous of *me*.

Nick resented how much easier relationships were for straight people. For me to go to a school volleyball game, have a crush on a girl, and then leave the volleyball game with a *different* girl crushing on me—to him, that was "normal." I never had to come out or go through the hardships of homophobia. The only thing blocking me was my own thoughts.

This was the first time I realized that my brothers aren't perfect. Especially Nick. I just never saw it because of the strong and caring mask he put on every day.

While Nick was sitting in the backseat of the car waiting for me to get out of the neuropsychologist, he was fighting inner battles I didn't know about. He'd known about his sexuality from an early age, maybe even as early as three or four years old, but his heart took way longer to connect to his brain.

Part of this had to do with us being triplets. For all his life, Nick used me and Chris to figure out which of his emotions were valid. If he felt a certain way about something, me and Chris had to feel that way too and vice versa. If we all weren't on the same page and didn't have the same exact experience, then that feeling must've been wrong. That was just the insane amount of pressure we put on each other.

The other half of this had to do with me specifically. My mom was by my side because I forced her to be, and for so long, I seemed to be the only one of her boys with any type of hardship. My problems were the only problems that mattered because mine were the only ones people could see. But nobody could see through the fact that Nick wasn't 100% himself yet. His coming out to me, Chris, and Nathan was a bigger step than I had ever taken in any of my mental health obstacles. And it is still one of the moments I am most proud of him for.

The first thing I said to him when he came out was, "I'm sorry." I had unknowingly taken our parents' attention for myself because of my anxiety. And worse, I wasn't there for him in the way I thought I should have been.

After a long conversation, I realized more about him than I ever knew. The courage that it took for him to come out was leaps and bounds ahead of any courage I had in myself. Sharing that had more of an impact on me than he will ever know. Our generation may be more accepting than others, but still, growing up gay couldn't have been easy. Even offhanded homophobic comments, jokes, and judgments, no matter the other person's intentions, gave Nick one message: You're different. And if his family or friends found out about that difference, it may have changed what they thought about him. That came with a lot of fear.

That's why he'd told some of his friends before us. We were jokingly mad at him, but ultimately understood that it's easier to tell a friend than it is to tell two people he would have to wake up and see every day, especially without knowing exactly how we'd react. After the house fire, being crammed into such a small space in that apartment, Nick would have to live out every second of our reactions in real time. Even if we didn't respond negatively, just changing the way we acted around him at all could've been devastating.

Nothing changed for me, though.

All I wanted was for Nick to be himself.

Having his brothers' acceptance, he later came out to the rest of our family. Then, publicly, during COVID. Now, as time goes on, I see him grow more and more into his skin. He was my awakening to a new thought process: I'm not the only person with challenges in life to figure out. Silent battles, like Nick's, or loud battles, like screaming in the passenger seat of my mom's minivan, are equally important. The only difference was that while growing up, I had a team of people trying to reboot my brain and find solutions for my problems. But he was going through a mental battle alone.

All Nick has ever shown me—before and after coming out—is strength.

He gave me hope that, eventually, I could be strong too.

Want to Go for a Drive?

Within the first two months of sophomore year, Nick started working at Star Market, a local grocery store where our mom had worked from 16 to 22 years old. All the kids around us were now old enough to get jobs and pay for snacks at school or movie tickets, but I couldn't do it yet. I viewed working the same as school, the only difference being that I would get paid for it. Well, and the fact that I would be relied on more. At school, I could miss a day or hide in the bathroom without affecting anyone but myself and my own grades. The class would move on without me. But if I flaked while working under a manager, I'd probably create extra work for my coworkers or get fired. So, Nick, who wanted the extra money, had to be the guinea pig.

The plan was for Nick to get the job and then tell me and Chris if it was worth applying for. About five or six months into Nick working there, he gave us the go-ahead: He liked his co-workers, and with it being one of the smallest grocery stores in the city, it only ever got busy during rush hour. By the end of sophomore year, I applied. The Star Market manager was the aunt of our childhood best friend, so she put a good word in for me and Chris. Nick was one of the best employees they had, so they figured that we would be good workers too. I didn't even have an interview. Instead, I just filled out a couple of work safety forms, and before I knew it, I was in front of a register.

Even though I didn't want to work at all, I still gave it a shot because of Nick. Having school during the week meant we all worked weekends, so our schedules naturally overlapped. Nick trained me and taught me how to type in certain fruits and vegetables and how to reprint a receipt. The best part about working with family was that they understood me. Nick or Chris would cover me if I needed an extra break in the bathroom to calm down, or they would let me shut off my register and bag groceries for them if I needed to. Sometimes, the feeling of being trapped behind a register would get to me. That feeling of "I cannot move until I scan every single one of this person's items . . . and then the person behind them . . . and then the next person after that" would slowly make me lose my mind as more and more customers joined the line. At school, I felt trapped by the building itself, but at work, I was trapped by obligation—the understanding that if I up and left, I'd be inconveniencing a ton of people.

Apart from the trapped feeling, the work was otherwise manageable. Star Market was a low-key grocery store, minus the time between five and seven o'clock when it filled with so many people, I'd think the building might explode. Also, minus the typical crazy people you help when working any customer service job. Some of our regulars included:

- a woman who was so scared of technology, she would freak out if you used your phone instead of a calculator;
- a man who came in with a hiker's backpack and only bought canned goods, which made us think he was prepping for the apocalypse; and
- another man who tried to return a case of sodas that he'd clearly drunk and then filled back up with water.

Maybe my favorite story, though, is when a customer once reached into the live lobster tank with his bare hands and stuck a lobster on my conveyor belt, confused as to why I couldn't just scan a live animal and why he had to get it weighed and bagged at the deli first.

How certain people can go through life not reading signs or understanding what's going on at all was just crazy to me. Telling someone their coupon expired was like telling them a loved one had died. The extent that people would go to save even 50 cents or a dollar shocked me, but that's also why I'm glad I worked retail when I did. For the first time, I looked into the real world, into what life could be like after I graduated. I also learned the importance of a dollar, which is what motivated me when I had to work four to five days a week during my summer break. More money equaled more candy, soda, and Fortnite V-Bucks.

I never really loved Star Market, but I eventually became comfortable there—or comfortable enough. I knew its layout, which aisles and corners of the store I could walk down to avoid the gazes of fellow employees and customers. This wasn't necessarily the case at school anymore.

During my first year of high school, what I *thought* would be the worst thing ever happened: The city put my high school under construction.

A fully new school would be built about 400 feet away, and certain wings of our current building would be remodeled too. I spent the whole school year memorizing the building, only for it to be torn apart, demolished, and put back up. I would have new classrooms, bathrooms, and hiding spots to learn all over again.

Before starting construction, the workers built the "mod," a long, one-story building with temporary classrooms outside of the real high school. Luckily, none of my classrooms were affected or would have to move until the next year, but I wasn't excited for that whatsoever.

By sophomore year, not only did it take me longer to learn the way to my classes and my certain routes, but once I was in the classroom, all the lessons would be interrupted by drilling and the *beep-beep-beep* of forklifts reversing. Sometimes, the floors would shake from the jackhammering. For that entire year, I felt like I needed a hard hat and safety vest just to study.

The construction only got worse during my junior year. Our carpentry class was in a different school, and my gym class was at a church that had a basketball court in the basement, so we had to take buses in the middle of the day to some classes. The only side benefit was an endless number of excuses. Since the classrooms were further away and certain hallways were blocked off, I could spend more time in the bathroom, show up late for class, and blame fallen rocks or bricks for being in the way.

Again, the construction is what I *thought* was the worst possible scenario. What I didn't know was that, soon, I wouldn't need to avoid being in a classroom . . . because there would be no school to go to.

I vividly remember the day before the COVID-19 lockdown: March 12, 2020.

I had skipped gym to sit in Nick and Chris's English class. The English teacher was very chill. Even though I did not have her class, she was fine with me sitting in and didn't question anything. She even let Chris keep Pepsi in her mini fridge and walk in whenever he wanted to grab one. That day, I remember her standing in front of the class and explaining why, for weeks, people had started to wear masks everywhere and were calling out of school and work sick. COVID felt like the flu, but wasn't, she explained. We would likely have two weeks off school, and then we'd be right back at it.

When everyone left school that day, our group went to Nathan's house. After a little while, we bought movie tickets, walked around the nearby shopping center, and grabbed burritos and tacos at a Mexican restaurant. We did this all the time, but that day, it was

. . . *eerie*. There was no one else around. We went to the movie, and the entire theater was empty except for us. Not wanting to go home, we were walking around the shopping center some more when Nathan showed everyone a post on Instagram from a local news account: The first positive case of COVID-19 in Somerville was confirmed earlier that day. And the person likely contracted it while in the same shopping center where we were walking around.

Horrified, we all practically ran back to Nathan's and then parted ways back to our own homes. Two weeks later, when the English teacher said we'd be back in school, the lockdown hit. Everyone had to stay home, and if you went out for essentials, you had to social distance—meaning stay six feet away from anyone you didn't live with—and wear a medical mask to reduce the likelihood of passing COVID on to someone else.

I was devastated.

Somehow, when summer ended and school started, I walked into my junior year of high school not anxious at all—the first time that had happened since seventh grade. I made three very solid friends aside from Nathan, and I had a lot of friends through Nick and in classes at school. I didn't have to worry about sports I didn't truly love. I was back to only working on the weekends. And even though I hated the apartment, I was only a five-minute walk away from school. I was truly starting to become who I wanted to be.

I pretty much felt unstoppable. I was getting comfortable with school for the first time, spending time with people I loved instead of hiding in my room, and working toward my license. Everything was going according to plan—but then COVID went and ruined it.

After years of trapping myself in my house because of my own paranoia and anxiety, the second I started to make progress, I had to stay home. Where I used to find my comfort, I was now in a cage.

I was unwillingly reliving my middle school lifestyle that I hated so much.

I switched to online school after the first two weeks of the pandemic. I'm not joking when I say that during the last quarter of junior year, I logged into one online class per day, and that was it. I thought it was absolutely ridiculous. I woke up, turned on a laptop screen, pretended I was listening to the teacher talk, answered to my name for attendance, and then played Fortnite for six hours. That was the easiest quarter of school in my life. I didn't do a single thing, and they somehow passed me.

Beyond that, my timeline for COVID feels a little off because of how repetitive the days got during summer break. I picked up more shifts at Star Market, and that's when I started to see all the cleaning supplies and toilet paper fly off the shelves. Masks became more and more common as weeks went by. Once it started to feel like COVID wasn't slowing down, me, Nick, and Chris stopped going to work. To be honest, I don't even remember quitting. I guess Nick just called our manager and told her we'd take a leave because we didn't want to risk catching COVID. But we were young, and it was still summertime. We knew that Star Market wouldn't be our jobs forever. After that, I never worked another Star Market shift again.

With no job and no school, I played Fortnite until the sun came up. Me and Chris were nocturnal. We would play and scream at our screens and wake up our parents, who were two rooms over with a very normal sleep schedule, in the middle of the night, and they would come in and yell at us to be quiet. I was in the wrong, waking them up, but I also had nothing else to do. I fell into a trap of video games.

The days we did spend outside felt odd, though. Everything was touched by the pandemic in some way. On August 1, 2020, me,

Nick, and Chris celebrated our 17th birthday at Chuck E. Cheese—not to play in the arcade (not that we could anyway because of social distancing) but because they were still selling food to keep the business going during COVID. So, we spent the day eating Dippin' Dots in the car. Not the most eventful birthday, but still fun.

When school started back up, I had to wake up to log on to Zoom calls. I would still stay up until three in the morning, but join our classes at seven. I would fall asleep in lessons and wake up to being in random breakout rooms with extra-help teachers asking if I needed them. I would say no and then go back to sleep.

I was unhealthy, not sleeping a normal amount. I constantly stared at screens, either on my phone for homework or playing video games. Some days, I only left my bed to use the bathroom. I joined school from under my comforter, turned my camera off, and watched *Stranger Things* or *Outer Banks* until it was time for bed again. I ate candy and soda during the day and DoorDash'd fast food for dinner. I was a mess. I hadn't been in sunlight for weeks. I knew that I had to get better, but I found comfort in doing nothing. When I wasn't in school, I was FaceTiming with my friends, who I missed a lot. FaceTime was also the only way I could talk to the girl I liked. She confessed that she also liked me, but because of COVID, we couldn't do anything about it, besides just talking on the phone.

I missed my house. I missed my family's old routine. Any sense of privacy would've also been nice. The apartment had a weird layout, like it was specifically designed to be as claustrophobic as humanly possible. The floor plan was almost a perfect square, with Nick's room all the way in the back, the living room and dining room (where me and Chris slept) to the left of the front door, and Justin and my parents' bedrooms to the right. If you wanted to enter a certain room, you had to walk through several other rooms to get there. For example, if Nick wanted to get to his room, he had to either walk through Justin's room or he had to shove past me and Chris in the dining room. With six people and a dog jammed into a two-bedroom apartment, it was total chaos. At the beginning, we thought we'd get used to it, especially since me and my brothers spent a lot of time out of the house. But COVID made that impossible.

The apartment was a comfort to my mom, though. We were renting from an older Portuguese couple who lived on the first floor of the building. In a "small world" moment, the wife realized that she knew my great-grandmother and aunt from Portugal and even used to see my mom as a little girl getting her hair cut at the local barber. Once we moved in, the couple would check in on us and cook us Portuguese food—and my mom felt like young MaryLou again, being comforted by her grandparents. The tight layout of the apartment was also a slight comfort to my mom: She always knew where her babies were.

We didn't feel the same way.

The complete lack of personal space caused tensions to run high the whole two years we lived on top of each other. Everyone got mad over the smallest things. My dad came home from work around 11 every night and turned on the TV in the living room. He wanted to watch TV until one in the morning when me and Chris, who slept only a few feet away, had to be up at seven for school. Every night he did this was another screaming match, with me and Chris shouting, "You can't be doing this anymore! The house isn't big enough!" Ironically, we were fighting over us losing sleep but, in the process, probably waking up everybody else in the apartment with our yelling. And it's not like we would have even gone to sleep at that time anyway. The frustration came from the principle of it. There was no privacy, and having to constantly compete over whose phone call, TV show, or video game was the loudest quickly got old. With all of us being crammed together with zero downtime, the apartment became a warzone.

Out of my entire family, my relationship with Nick probably took the worst hit.

I will be the bigger person here and admit that I was very annoying.

Chris's and my lifestyles synced. We hardly ever argued because we spent the lockdown playing video games together. But Nick didn't play them at all unless he wanted to talk to Nathan on the headset. He spent most of his time in his room, talking to friends on the phone or planning different photography projects. When the days started running together, I'd pick the lock to his room and barge in to jump on his bed or put on his clothes. Sometimes I'd rearrange his camera stuff and take pictures of myself, him, or whatever was around. If he were on FaceTime, I'd scream "Hi!" to his friends. It was very fair to say that I was invading his personal space and getting on his nerves, and what started as basic sibling fights turned into constant screaming matches. The anger wasn't playful or funny; it was real and stuck around. But these arguments became a way for me to break up the crazy and unhealthy cycle we all found ourselves in. Whenever I got sick of doing the same thing at the same time every single day, the solution became barging into Nick's room to steal something.

As triplets, me, Nick, and Chris had been in close proximity to each other for basically our entire lives. But it was the *forced* proximity that tested our relationship to the max. In such a confined space, there was no way to avoid a problem or hide until you or the other person calmed down. If someone was upset, you could see it on their face.

Confrontation became a part of everyday life. Me, Nick, and Chris would literally get into a huge fight, want to escape the pressure cooker that was our apartment, and then leave together, still arguing. Like full-on screaming at each other one minute and then, the next, asking, "Want to grab McDonald's?" The other person would respond, "Yeah, let me get my jacket." And we'd be sitting in the car, pissed off and eating our food in the parking lot.

During all this, my mom was still going out every day to shop for families from her school who were struggling during the pandemic. But at night, she didn't need the minivan, so I could use it.

Before COVID, we found every possible way to be out of the house. Now that I could drive, that opportunity opened up again.

My Perfect Life?

I don't know how it started, but every night from 9 to 11 p.m., me, Nick, and Chris started driving to our old house, which had just been given the go-ahead for rebuilding. What should have been a three-to-six-month project *in total* had now taken seven months *just to secure permits.* Then, of course, as soon as they were finally ready to start repairs, COVID paused construction too. Only two people could work on our house at a time, and they had to social distance with one floor between them. Building a house takes way more than two people; so many projects require two sets of hands. But this would have to be the protocol until COVID ended, and since no one could predict when that would happen, we had no idea when we'd get our house back.

Some days, it looked like the construction workers had ripped up the floors or brought in new materials. Other days, it was obvious they hadn't worked at all. After walking around from room to room to see the progress, we would just sit on the kitchen floor and talk for hours. We spent every waking moment together, caged in a small apartment, but for some reason, we were only able to really talk there, surrounded by what remained of our burnt childhood home.

When I say we took these mini rides and had conversations every night, I mean it. Me and Chris played video games all day during school hours. By the time my mom came home from work at night, our eyes would be burning from the screen. Just to escape the brain fog, we would go on walks to the nearby park, sit on the swings, talk for hours, leave the swings, walk up the hill, sit in the grass to talk more, and then drive to the burnt house, only to talk even more. We never stopped finding words to say.

The conversations were all over the place—the good, the bad, and everything in between. I explained to them how it was hard for me to be locked in the house when I just started to feel better, how I missed my friends, how I wished I had more time with the girl I liked, and how any new friends I made would never be able to see the house I grew up in.

Nick talked about how it was hard for him to come out and how it was so new. He called me out on pissing him off and blaming him when I was the one running into his space and causing chaos. Chris mostly had the same worries as me: He missed Nathan and our other friends, and even though he knew he loved music, he had no idea what to do for his future. Just that college was not an option.

Complaining about school and COVID and stress, we solved problems with each other and talked on a deeper emotional level than before. But more than anything, we told stories from the past. Like the time Chris flipped over our friend's shoulders one year, trying to climb a tree while apple-picking. Or the time Nick threw down his gloves because he was so mad when playing hockey for the first time. To end the night, we drove to McDonald's, Burger King, or some fast food place to go through the drive-thru and stuff our faces in the parking lot, continuing our conversations from earlier.

We cried laughing all night and looked forward to the next night—or at least, I did. I couldn't wait for every day to end, just so I could drive at midnight when the roads and sidewalks were clear. When we had free rein to go anywhere we wanted, but chose our old house again and again anyway. When it felt like we were the only three people left on Earth.

And when all that mattered was making each other laugh—me driving, Chris in the passenger seat, and Nick in the back.

With our nightly drives and conversations came a lot of talk about our passions and the future. Nick had dreams to go to Salem State University for photography and video editing, but I realized right away that college wasn't for me. Going to a school without my brothers seemed impossible. I wouldn't even know how to start making friends or how to pick a major on my own.

Chris also didn't want to go to college, but thought he would probably go into the carpenter's union. I didn't want to do that either. Whatever little spark I had for carpentry was done. COVID ruined my chances of doing hands-on work during school and readying myself for a real carpentry job. You can talk about building all you want online, but actually doing the work was much different.

One night, after coming back from one of those drives, I stayed up until sunrise and climbed over Nick's mattress and through his window onto the front porch. My day had looked the same as every other day that month: I played video games until my brain was fried and the backs of my eyes ached in my head. I ordered the usual food from DoorDash and ate it without tasting anything, just shoving calories in my face out of obligation. I had probably irritated Nick or Chris at least once that day, or they had irritated me, one of the two. Somehow, in a house of five other people, I felt alone. The days had started to blend, and time existed in a sort of limbo, like COVID created a space in between living and simply existing.

I dropped to the floor of the porch and rolled on my back. The rising sun felt hotter than normal, but that was probably because this was my first time getting any real vitamin D in months. It was so early that the birds weren't even awake, so once again, I had a similar feeling as when me, Nick, and Chris went out at night and there were no people on the streets: an eerie apocalyptic feeling that I was the only one left on the planet.

In the stillness, I thought about what life had become for me. So many times, I woke up in the middle of the day, thinking it was nighttime. At late hours, when video games and TV bored me, I zoned out and concentrated on the same questions: Who would I be if I had no mental problems, no COVID, and no school? What did my perfect life look like? Would I go to college? Would I join the carpenter's union right away?

I didn't know.

I'd be turning 18 soon, and I didn't have a plan. Once the summer ended, I had a decision to make: carpenter's union, which I'd hate, or college, which I'd aimlessly go into debt for with no real goals or intentions. But at least I'd be doing *something*.

I pushed these thoughts to the very back of my mind, figuring I at least had some time to think about it. All I wanted to focus on was having a good summer and, once I turned 18, buying a scratch-off for the first time.

Where Do I Go from Here?

Me, Nick, and Chris have always loved to film videos, even as kids. Nick especially gravitated toward photography. My mom had photo albums and scrapbooks from before we were born, and she made one for every single year, capturing every event in her life and ours. Starting in the fourth grade, Nick would take her camera and snap photos of the family, wanting to help make the scrapbooks. When we got a little older, Nathan's mom gave him a higher-end camera that also shot video and showed him how to use it.

Originally, we made fake movie trailers using our iPod and edited them together on iMovie, and that slowly built into posting longer videos on YouTube. The first videos of us were mostly vlogs of our family trips, posted to Nick's personal channel. But there were also videos of Chris putting shaving cream in his hand and smacking someone across the face, and another one where we put a friend in a tire and rolled him down his driveway, watching him dramatically fall out of it once he hit a fence. We also watched a lot of FailArmy. In most of those videos, someone is hit by something, or they trip and fall—basically, someone gets injured in a weird way. So, we tried to stage "fails" ourselves, but wanting to make the video super realistic, we usually ended up *actually* hurting ourselves.

Around 2011, the most popular YouTube videos involved some level of "punishment" or prank, like the cinnamon challenge. That kind of content stuck with us. Years later, one of our first videos on our combined channel was quizzing Justin on how much he knew about the three of us, and then whichever triplet he knew the least had to wax off their leg hair. I vividly remember Chris's screams as Justin ripped the strip of hair off his leg.

Essentially, we've been filming videos our entire lives. It's just that COVID reminded us of how much we loved it. Since we were stuck playing video games in the house anyway, me and Chris figured we should start streaming on Twitch, which only made our screen time worse. Because we lived in such a small apartment, we had to wait for our mom and dad to go to bed if we wanted to stream, since we didn't want to be arguing on a live feed only for our parents to come in and tell us to go to bed. Building an audience when you exclusively stream at three in the morning isn't easy. Our chat was only Europeans and the few people who stayed up all night to watch us.

Video games eventually got old, though, to the point where I was sick and tired of staring at a screen all day, every day. The only time we ever seemed to have any real fun was on drives to our childhood home and then to McDonald's afterward, sitting in the parking lot and talking for hours. Our conversations went all over the place, sometimes taking dark turns to very deep emotions, but then pivoting back to topics like whether we believed in mermaids or not. I don't remember whose idea it was, but it makes sense that our next move was to start filming the car talks and posting them to YouTube.

At first, we wanted to record our lives so we could show our kids one day. But eventually, "it'd be cool to show our kids what we were like in high school" turned into "it'd be insane for them to see what life was like during a global pandemic." For the entirety of COVID, we filmed everything we could: playing games with Justin, behind-the-scenes shots of Nick's at-home photoshoots, and our late-night conversations in the car. Our love for making videos was back. Even better, we could make whatever we wanted without live reactions from critics at school. Anyone who could make fun of us for "corny" or "cringy" content was locked in their house, just like us. This freedom was huge, especially because now I realize: Any great idea is going to be seen as crazy or weird until it's a success.

Even though Nick showed way more interest in TikTok, Chris started making short videos on there during COVID, having nothing else to do, and built a following of over 60,000 people. He pulled me and Nick into it, and we made one video where we all used Face ID to unlock the same phone. Since our faces are basically identical, it worked, even though commenters went crazy saying that we somehow faked it. That's when people started to find our videos. They didn't just scroll past without engaging—they were genuinely curious about our lives. Chris read comments out loud to us:

"Wait, there are two of them?"

"No, there are three!"

"Do you guys all have the same friends?"

"Do you share the same clothes?"

"Can you read each other's minds?"

We answered all these questions on our shared YouTube channel or on Chris's TikTok: "Yes, there are three of us. We do have a lot of the same friends, and we do steal each other's clothes sometimes, even though we sort of have different styles."

It wasn't long until Chris noticed that all of his TikTok videos got more views when we posted together. He had the idea that we should start a joint TikTok account, just like our YouTube. That night, we made the Sturinolo Triplets TikTok, where we mainly posted triplet-related content. In one video, we all argued about who was who in an old family photo of the three of us. In another, we weighed the pros and cons of being triplets, saying how it sucks when you're about to leave the house and can't figure out which pair of identical Air Force 1s is yours. On the day we posted our first video, we got 60,000 followers almost immediately. We couldn't believe it.

Despite TikTok being the easier platform, the goal was always to invest in our YouTube presence. We wanted to build a strong community of people who would watch long-form content and relate to us, not make quick 30-second videos for people to smile at and then scroll past, continuing on with the rest of their lives without even looking at our username. Therefore, to point viewers to the channel, we finished all of our TikToks with a message that full versions and more answers could be found on our YouTube. We didn't have a production schedule or any kind of organized "brand." All we knew was that we were having fun, and maybe, one day, we could make a little money off it.

YouTube and TikTok distracted us from COVID and the apartment, and because of these new goals we had, we somehow didn't totally lose our minds. By the time COVID cases started to drop in number and more people became vaccinated, the repairs to our old house also sped up. One night, all the two-by-fours would be drilled in, and another night, more wires would be installed in the wall. More and more progress was being made during the day, whereas before, full days would pass without any new work to see.

By January 23, 2021, we had officially moved back in—a weird feeling. The kitchen had a brand-new island and marble countertops, and a full wall was taken out, removing the closet and hallway to make space for Nick's new room. Even though I was grateful to finally be home, a part of me felt like it was missing. I had trouble getting used to this new house since all my memories were in the old one.

Slowly, the world opened back up. After a year of talking, I finally asked out the girl I liked. Before COVID, I was too nervous to ask, so I used COVID as an excuse to delay it. Her strict dad also made me hesitant. When we went out to the movies or to hang out at Nathan's, he insisted she be home before sunset, and I was never allowed inside her house. It's no surprise that when school started back up, her dad didn't want her to attend in person, so I still couldn't see her at all.

On March 18, 2021, in-person school started again, but only from 8 a.m. to 12 p.m. All the desks were pushed six feet apart, and masks were mandated. Most of our time was spent in carpentry class, but it's not like anyone could be close enough to each other to help build anything. Luckily, since me and Chris lived together, our teachers let us build Adirondack chairs— those wooden lounge chairs you see on patios—together as a project.

School turned into an even bigger waste of time, but I was too burnt out from my former apartment life to have much anxiety about it. I knew I would pass as long as I kept showing up. That's all anybody really cared about. Plus, most of the day was taken up by in-school COVID testing and chilling in our shop class. The majority of what gave me anxiety wasn't even a part of my day anymore. My two biggest concerns became graduating in two months and working on social media. With any success there, I wouldn't have to go into the carpenter's union.

Growing up, I figured I would become someone who once helped me. Maybe a teacher, firefighter, or therapist. Sitting in Jessie's office, I remember thinking all the time, *She's not saying what I would say right now. If I were a therapist, I would know exactly how to help myself.* I couldn't see how her advice would impact my life, and she made the whole therapy thing seem like a lost cause. In her shoes, I'd understand my patients' situations, having been in that spot myself. I know what it's like on the other side of the desk, telling a total stranger your deepest fears and insecurities and expecting, but not always receiving, a way out.

But that dream quickly fizzled once I knew I wasn't going to college and earning a degree, let alone a master's degree. My experience in school had shown me that I hated everything about the structure, meeting new people, talking to teachers, and doing all the homework. After high school, I would need a decent-paying job, but my only real experience was in carpentry. It was a viable option, but I had zero enjoyment in it anymore. Unlike making videos with my brothers.

I did as much work as I needed to pass for the year and hung out with my friends every day until May 21, my last day of school ever. Now it was time to work on YouTube. The three of us graduated on June 7, 2021. We were at 25,000 YouTube subscribers, a number that kept growing every day.

Like any aspiring influencer, Nick made an email to put in our bio for any type of business inquiries. Just five days after our last day of high school, we were signed to a manager in LA who offered us a million different opportunities, including flying out to LA for the first time in our lives. I knew nothing about business, but I was excited to learn.

I hadn't seen my girlfriend in a month because I was spending all of my time with my brothers and focusing on graduating. She called me and told me to stop by her grandparents' house so I could see her before leaving for California. When I pulled up in front of the house the next day, she walked out to the car, hopped into the passenger seat, and looked at me. I could tell something wasn't right.

She immediately started crying and put her head in her lap. I asked her what was wrong.

"I don't want you to be mad because none of it is your fault," she said. I expected where this was going. She then explained to me that her best friend was moving 40 minutes away to a different city. Her grandpa wasn't doing well. She felt lost. And ultimately, she broke up with me to focus on the challenges in her life.

I rubbed her back and told her that it was okay and not to be upset. I understood completely. I was going to LA in three days to try and pursue my dream job. She was going through a lot, and family was everything to her. She needed to focus on that.

I viewed this as a new beginning for both of us. There was never any bad blood, and I still care about her.

Days later, I sat in the airport, waiting for our flight to California. With COVID still a threat, everyone was either wearing blue surgical masks or patterned fabric masks they'd bought online. My mom came with us because (1) I couldn't have gone without her, but also (2) she didn't know what we were getting into and wanted to make sure we were safe. The fact that her sons' YouTube channel was growing so much that they now needed a Hollywood manager, in a matter of months, seemed too good to be true. Any on-top-of-it parent would think that was a little sketchy.

As much as the week in LA was a "work trip," we had so much fun. LA was way bigger than Boston, with a lot more people, traffic, and heat. Our manager spent time with our mom, telling her all about herself and her goals for us. We bowled, went out to eat, and had photoshoots. The week went by fast, but we still got an exciting glimpse into what our futures could look like. I envisioned myself living in LA one day, although I thought that day would come years and years later.

All I could think about was how, a year prior, me and my brothers had been working at a grocery store. Now, our lives were about to completely change.

100K

100,000 Subscribers?

One of my family's traditions is going to my godmother Tina's house in Maine for Labor Day weekend. I loved going there so much. All of my mom's friends from when she worked at Star Market, with all of their husbands and kids, would come together for the trip. I rarely saw these people outside of this holiday weekend, but for years, it was the most fun I would have all summer long.

We could never count on the cell service, and we only had WiFi available inside the house, so all the kids spent time playing games outside like capture the flag and manhunt. When we were exhausted from running around, there was a tire swing, rope swing, and hammock. My favorite part was riding the old-school bikes and skateboards they stored in a shed in the backyard. We'd all choose a bike and then ride to the beach. Whenever we were hungry, we stopped at the seaside store to buy chicken fingers, french fries, and Slush Puppies before heading back, waiting to see whose bike chain would fall off first. I remember laughing as we'd stop to let them put their chain back on, then race back to my godmother's house with our food. Evenings were spent around the campfire telling stories, with Tina's husband cracking jokes. All the kids would hear their parents tell stories about them that they had never heard before.

My godmother is an amazing woman. Out of everyone who went to her house, I was happiest to see her. Tina was a familiar face in the crowd at our hockey games, and every year when we were little, she would take me and my brothers out to the movies for our birthday. When Christmas came around, she always gave me, her godson, an ornament with my name on it, while Nick and Chris got candy. Her son and daughter were both closer to our brother Justin's age, so it was difficult getting to know them at first, but as we've gotten older, we've come to relate to each other. They feel like family.

The Labor Day weekend after high school was different than any before. As the last night wound down, the fire went out, and everybody started going to bed. Me, Nick, and Chris weren't tired and went upstairs to hang out in the living room. My mom and Tina followed us up.

This being the last weekend of the summer, all the college kids had to leave a day early to go back to school for the year. But obviously, me and my brothers stayed in Maine. High school was over, we were no longer working at Star Market, and we didn't have any solid plans of going to college—not even Nick, who, before, was deadset on Salem.

In the living room, my mom, Tina, and my brothers talked about nothing for a while. It's like we were all skirting around the elephant in the room. Everyone knew me, Nick, and Chris were taking our YouTube videos seriously, but we could tell people were thinking, *They're probably not going to be able to do this*. Sure, we were already making some money, but it was anywhere between $150 and $300 a month. This was not nearly enough to support one career, let alone three. Nobody wanted to be the one to crush our dreams. We made it clear, though: Our goal was YouTube.

I could count on my godmother to guide me in the right direction and look out for my best interests. She and my mom had concerns about us not going to college. They didn't want us to put all of our focus on YouTube, only for it to be a waste of time, so they were very adamant that we each have a backup plan. The possibility of failing was hard to hear, but we understood the reality of our situation. It was make or break.

We had way too much hope to give up. Over the summer, we watched our subscriber count rise from 25,000 to 37,000. In just a few months, 12,000 people had found our channel. We wanted to keep growing, but it would take a lot of work.

We ended the conversation with them by making a deal. We were allowed to take a gap year to see where YouTube could get us. If we didn't have 100,000 subscribers by the following Labor Day, me and Chris had to go into carpentry, and Nick had to enroll in college. We left Maine that next morning with every intention of coming back next year as full-time YouTubers. There was nothing we wanted more—we had never been so motivated. If we wanted this to be a job, then we had to take it all more seriously.

When we returned to Boston, our manager and friends from LA came to visit. We hit it off so well in LA that we wanted to share our hometown with them. While they visited, they met all of our oldest friends. We went to the local basketball courts, where we would meet to talk and skateboard. Our Boston friends thought our friends from LA were so cool and made jokes about hating Massachusetts. They were especially jealous of the weather they got to experience every day. After our LA friends went back home, we spent the rest of the summer nights either filming our videos or hanging out at the basketball courts with our local friends. We would have deep life conversations about people's family lives, jobs, what college people were going to—we talked about everything until the lights on the court shut off for the night.

As summer turned to fall, me, Nick, and Chris went back to the basketball courts like always . . . but it was a weird feeling. Some of our friends weren't there because they had left for college, they had work in the morning, or they had high school the next day. The friends who were there had no idea what they wanted to do with their lives. All they knew was that, like us, they didn't want to go to college.

I think leaving high school and picking a new path is one of the most stressful things a young person has to go through. Personally, the initial change of routine horrified me. I was choosing to live part of my life in California, where I only had a couple of friends and didn't know any of the local shops, bathrooms, hospitals, or anything. My anxiety was creeping up.

What motivated me the most during this time was my brothers. I believed and trusted them more than anyone else. If we weren't doing it together, I would have had no desire to put any part of my life on social media. Without them, instead of packing to spend another month in LA, I would have been in downtown Boston with a hard hat, sawing wood.

We returned to LA at the end of October, with plans to stay at our manager's house for a few reasons. For starters, we couldn't afford to stay in a hotel for a month with our couple-hundred-dollars-a-month income from YouTube. But the most important reason was that our mom had entrusted us with our manager. Under her supervision, we were much safer than we would be living on our own. People didn't understand our relationship or understand why we were so close with our management team, but we saw friendship before we saw business. That trust allowed us to work together as a team. It's a very unique situation when you find people you know you can rely on. For us, it was instantaneous; we all had each other's best interests from the start, and our relationship never felt like work. Fun came first, and serious meetings were reserved for when we had to get real work done. When we pictured our lives doing YouTube full-time, this was it.

When we were back in Boston, we spent as much time as we could with our friends, but working on our YouTube videos became the priority. We put a lot of effort into planning our shoots, even going as far as dumpster diving. My dad was working at the school one night and saw a teacher put a large classroom whiteboard in the trash, so Nick and Chris asked him to take it from the school's dumpster and put it in Chris's room. We used that whiteboard all the time, organizing all our channel's information. We had a list of about 50 video ideas at any given point and projected how many new subscribers we needed every month to meet our goal. As demands for merch grew, we also used it to plan clothing designs and brand names we liked.

We all fell into natural roles based on what we liked doing most. Nick, loving photography, figured out how to shoot and edit all of our videos, and he became kind of like our coordinator. Figuring that consistency was key, he put together a posting schedule for us: every Friday at 5:30 p.m. That way, kids would be notified of a new video right after school, and if they weren't able to watch it right away, they would have all weekend to see it.

For his job, Chris, being creative, came up with video ideas and topics for us to talk about in the car. Most of our early videos came from fan suggestions on Instagram, so we chose from those a lot of the time before turning to Chris's ideas.

As for me, I mostly just did what anybody told me to do. Even if I wanted to help edit, Nick didn't have the patience to teach me, instead yelling that he'd just do it faster.

We worked nonstop. A typical day looked like hanging out with our friends, and when they had to go get ready for school or work, that's when we went home to plan a video or went to the parking lot to film. We knew that when Thanksgiving rolled around, we wanted to be in Boston to spend time with our family.

The day before Thanksgiving, we hit 50,000 subscribers. With 10 months left to hit our goal, we were already halfway there. What an amazing time to be thankful. The coolest thing about our growth on YouTube and social media was that the more we were being ourselves on the internet, the faster we grew.

In the new year, it all happened. Our videos had been gaining traction. On January 5, 2022, we hit 100,000 subscribers. Our growth predictions were blown out of the water, and it became hard to keep track of exactly how many subscribers we gained every day. Maybe the most insane moment for me ever.

When anyone hits 100,000 subscribers on YouTube, the company sends them a creator award—a plaque for reaching that milestone. For me, that was proof that our hard work paid off. Reaching that goal was unbelievable, especially since we hit our goal with nine months to spare. Putting the plaque on my bedroom wall was my "I made it" moment. It didn't feel real. We were really gonna do it.

The crazy part was the rapid rate of growth. It just kept going. After three more months, we made it to a million subscribers. But in that amount of time, a lot more changed than just the subscriber count. As the months passed, the check from YouTube became bigger and bigger, and we realized that this could be a real, successful career for the three of us. One day, one of my favorite YouTubers followed us back on Instagram and offered for us to go on their podcast, *The CUFBOYS Show*, when we were back in LA. Me and Chris had been watching their videos since high school and looked up to them. They had inspired us to create our own videos. More and more, things I couldn't believe were happening every day.

Even before hitting 100,000 subscribers, we had been getting requests for merch. We were working on finding a company that could produce everything we wanted and had been brainstorming ideas for months. I came up with the name "Let's Trip" because it's "triplets" flipped around, and Nick and Chris loved it. We produced our first-ever merch drop two days after hitting a million subs. The day it dropped, I could not believe how many people bought it. Not only was I shocked by the amount of money made from our merchandise, but also by the number of people in different countries who liked our brand enough to buy it. It was hard to comprehend that my whole life had turned upside down in a matter of six months.

Apart from money and opportunities, a lot changed in my personal life too. My anxiety was masked, at first, by the excitement of what was going on, but even though I loved where my life was headed and everything we were doing, it slowly started to make its way back in.

Suddenly, in my hometown, I went to places I had been going to my whole life, but people started approaching me and asking for pictures. The first couple of times it happened, I was surprised and confused. I spent my life hiding myself as much as I could and blending in with everyone else. Getting attention was one thing over the internet, but in person, I hated all the eyes trained on me. This was a huge change of pace. One time, I saw an old school friend's little sister, and she spoke like she knew everything about me. Excited, she asked to take a picture with me, which I found a little weird. This wasn't the first time she had met me—she was probably at my birthday party when she was a kid. But she had really gotten to know me through our videos.

When I started on YouTube, I didn't realize the effect it would have on my real life. I didn't mind the pictures, but there would be the occasional crazy moments where strangers would show up at my home or I'd get followed around while driving my car. I didn't realize it at first, but it slowly started to turn me back to my old ways. I was scared someone would scream at me in public or that someone would follow me home and cause a car accident. All this anxiety caused me to stay home more. This new reality happened so fast that I could barely adjust to it.

A month after hitting 100,000, we hit 250,000.

A month after that, we hit 500,000.

By April, we had over a million subscribers.

By Labor Day—our deadline—we had three million.

I still had so much to learn about the world of social media and money management and life and relationships. It was hard making crazy decisions I never thought I'd have to make at 18 years old. And as much as that's true and as much as I had trouble adjusting to the suddenness of everything, I also finally knew what I wanted to do with my life.

Maybe the most validating fact was that, for my whole life, I struggled with being in front of people. I wanted to hide in the comfort of my own home and would have been totally okay with never leaving it again. New experiences, places, and people frightened me to the point of panic attacks, causing me to map out entire buildings before I felt the tiniest bit comfortable in them. And even then, I still counted the seconds until I could be home again.

I spent my childhood and teenage years feeling like I had no personality. I believed that whoever I was, I stole it from Justin, Nick, and Chris. My clothes, my hobbies, my whole identity—that wasn't mine; I was just copying my brothers. But when we started making YouTube videos, what shocked me was that people started identifying with me. For many, I'm their favorite out of the three.

Suddenly, the triplet with no personality had fans and supporters. And because of just that—who I am, separate from my brothers.

SOLD

What's the Mortgage?

When we were initially coming out to California, most people would think we were living the life, but the reality was much more down-to-earth. We were staying in the back half of our manager's garage, where she had put up a wall and door to make a separate room with a TV and three beds. It was comfy and convenient, and we were grateful we didn't have to pay for hotels, especially in the early days of the channel. But we knew from the experience of the apartment during COVID that we wouldn't last long living on top of each other. After our first merch drop, we started to talk about finding our own spot in LA.

It all happened so quickly.

We didn't even meet with a realtor or go into an open house. Chris was walking around a neighborhood we liked and saw a house being remodeled with a moving truck outside. He and our manager approached the movers and asked, "Is this house going up for sale?"

"It's supposed to be. It's going on the market in two weeks."

We toured the house, and it just felt right. The most important feature was that it had three bedrooms, each with its own bathroom.

Our manager helped us contact the owners directly, and we bought it before it ever made it to market. Because of our initial merch drop, we were able to take a page out of our grandfather's book and buy the house in cash. He couldn't stand renting and worked hard to buy his properties outright.

The process moved so fast . . . that our parents were the last ones to find out we bought a house. We told them over the phone that we no longer had to stay in the garage in LA, but it wasn't until we were back in Boston that our mom and dad started to ask more questions. The conversation started off casually, with us just sitting around talking in the living room like we usually do.

"It's a house in a great neighborhood. It has a big kitchen with three bedrooms."

"That's nice. How much are you paying a month for it?"

"Oh, we own it."

"But what are your monthly payments? What's the mortgage?"

"No, we bought the house in cash."

It dawned on my parents that their boys were leveling up faster than they thought. I'm sure they panicked a little, seeing their 18-year-old sons buy a house while my dad had two jobs and my mom still worked at the school. They worked hard all of our lives to feed four of us boys, and it wasn't lost on us that they had an entirely different relationship and perspective on money. My mom and dad are, by nature, giving people. It feels like for my entire childhood, my dad was picking up overtime or finding extra work to do, and for her whole life, prior to me and my brothers, my mom wanted to be a mother; she couldn't wait to take care of us. For us to sever that cord of financial dependence at such a young age . . . it was a scary and intimidating conversation to have.

Just because we didn't need our parents for financial help anymore didn't mean we wouldn't need them for every other kind of support, though. We explained that we would come back to Boston all the time—that no matter what happened, we would always come back—but for us to work on the YouTube channel, we needed a home base in California.

We did our best to reassure our parents that we weren't changing too quickly. We were still their children and wanted to support them as much as we could. Me, Nick, and Chris offered to pay the mortgage on their house, but they declined. They said that was our money. We needed to earn our own way.

But even though we were living our dream, I wasn't sure what my own way *was* yet.

We began the process of buying the house when we were 18 and finished signing off on it a couple of weeks after our 19th birthday—19 years old and living with my brothers on our own. This may have been the start of our life as "adults," but we were still kids at heart, learning how to mop and vacuum. My mom had taught us how to do chores, but I still had to call my manager and ask her to teach me how to work our washer and dryer when we first moved in. That's how I got stuck with becoming the laundry guy for my brothers and how we all naturally split tasks by what we were good at doing. Nick did the dishes, Chris handled the trash, and I washed and folded the laundry. What caused arguments was when Nick would let the plates pile up in the sink, or Chris would miss trash day. Or what still happens now: I pile all the freshly folded laundry on the stairs, and Nick, who's the worst, steps over it instead of taking it to his room, which makes me walk upstairs and throw the clothes all over his bed, making him refold them himself. Still, I'd rather do that than his job, where I'd have to touch wet food.

With the launch of merch, a healthy manager relationship, and a consistent content schedule, our career was in full effect. Like before, my excitement for this new journey in life masked all of my anxious thoughts and nervousness at first, but soon, the thought of living in LA full-time scared me. My parents and my best friend still lived in Boston. I knew, even though we planned to live in LA and work there for merch, events, and content, my heart was still with Boston. And it always will be.

When I got to this part of writing the book, I knew that I would struggle. I've had a lifetime to think about the past. But the present day? That's more complicated.

These last two years I've spent living in LA have been some of the most mature and developmental years of my life. Bits and pieces of these years are forever etched into the internet for the rest of time.

When moving out to LA, my anxiety didn't disappear like I thought it would—it evolved. My parents still lived in Boston and weren't able to help me with my every move, so my separation anxiety kicked into full gear. That attachment I once had with my mom and dad shifted to my brothers. I wouldn't go anywhere without Nick or Chris, to the point that I tagged along for plans that I didn't want to be a part of, just because I didn't want to Uber alone to join them somewhere later. Waking up in the morning, I would call for them, look around the house, and if I didn't see them, check their locations on my phone. Most roommates don't do that; they live their lives separately and then come home at the end of the day. But with us having the same schedule and the same days off, our lives became even more intertwined, if that was even possible.

With Nathan and all our basketball court friends back in Boston, though, I knew I would have to make an effort to make new friends. Typically, Nick and Chris did all the planning, and all I had to do was show up. Moving to LA felt like I was starting high school all over again, relying on my brothers to meet new people. For such a large part of my life, I was mad at myself for letting my anxious thoughts control me. I became more and more frustrated at the fact that life in LA felt like I took a few steps back.

As my life changed in California, so did my life back home in Massachusetts. I spent most of my time in Boston with my family and Nathan, but of course, I had other friends from high school as well. People say friends come and go in life, but I never believed it. Once I get to know someone and share a part of my life with them, I never want them not to be in my life. I couldn't imagine it. But what sucked about leaving high school was that it really showed me what friends I had only because we shared the same school. I lost a lot of friendships, not because of arguments or falling outs, but because they ended up going to college or moving out of the city after graduation. People's lives changed, and we all started our own journeys.

I missed late nights on the basketball courts. When we came home from LA, we brought a ton of great stories with us, but it wasn't long before we watched the basketball group slowly thin out as our friends had to leave early due to college or work the next morning. Before, we stayed out until the street lights went out, but now, we barely talked for a few hours and then, a lot of the time, not at all. Each time we went back to Boston, the distance between us and everyone else grew. Out of all the people I saw at the basketball court, I only ever hung out with a couple of them outside of the courts, and even though I was close to them, I knew that they were friends with the other guys more than with us. I never felt like any of my friendships ever ended. We just started to live our individual lives more.

All of us had trouble accepting reality—some of us more than others. I didn't want being in LA part-time to change the relationships I had for years. There's a part of me that feels guilty for moving away from home, but I was also starting to make amazing new friendships back in California, while they were all making new friends at college. I had believed that something crazy had to happen for a friendship to end, but in reality, it's normal and

I don't think anyone should feel bad for them ending. It's a part of maturing and realizing, as much as it sucks, we're not going to be in high school forever. I had to live my life, and they had to live theirs.

The only friend who could understand that we weren't going to LA to start a new life and abandon everyone was Nathan. He saw the value in true friendship and support, and I saw it in him. I already assumed, but that's when it was *confirmed* he would be in my life forever. If I didn't talk to Nathan for 10 years, I could go back to him, and we would pick up right where we left off. Not like we'd ever make it to 10 years, though, because the only goal within our friendship was to be there for each other in every moment, good and bad. When I think of Nathan, I think of how lucky I was to meet a once-in-a-lifetime friend like him. I never felt like I needed a million friends. I had my family, Nathan, and my new friends in California, and I was okay with that.

With planning my future and spending more time in LA, I attempted to get out of my comfort zone and meet new people. Once again, I didn't do a great job on my own, but I did much better when it came to groups. Nick and Chris started setting up more plans, and I always got along with at least one person out of the many they introduced me to. Starting these new friendships helped me with my separation anxiety from Nick and Chris, and slowly, I started to see myself doing more as an individual.

Except for driving in LA. I still couldn't do that.

SHO

How Do I Breathe Again?

I learned how to breathe right at 17 years old during my online gym class.

Because of COVID, Chris's and my high school gym class turned into more of a virtual health seminar. Since we couldn't exactly run laps around the track or play basketball together over Zoom, the PE teacher, Mrs. Munroe, gave us a lot of packets on the body. A couple of those packets had to do with heart rate and breathing.

A normal resting heart rate is between 60 and 100 beats per minute, but your heart rate increases as you exercise since the heart has to work harder to pump more blood. To see this for ourselves, the assignment was to check our resting pulse rate by pressing our fingers under our jaws and counting the beats per minute, write that down, and then do pushups or jumping jacks to see how much it went up. But gym was one of the classes that me and Chris slept through, so with eight minutes left, I would watch as Chris took his pulse and then quickly did as many pushups as he could in a minute. I didn't get that far, though. I just waited until Chris wrote down whatever his heart rate was after exercise and took off three or four points for my own packet.

Even if I didn't do the actual assignment, learning about my heart rate revealed a lot about anxiety. Just sitting around and doing nothing, my heart rate would sometimes be as high as Chris's was after he did all those pushups. The same thing happened when Mrs. Munroe taught us about breathing.

"Dude, you're not breathing right!" Chris laughed. "You need to figure this out!"

Mrs. Munroe was trying to teach us about box breathing, where you inhale, hold, exhale, and hold again for four seconds each. Except focusing on my breath was making me inhale and exhale weird. Kind of like how you can always see your nose but you don't really notice it until you focus, I couldn't breathe right once I became too conscious of it. Chris could do the assignment normally, but I kept almost hyperventilating—something I've struggled with all my life.

Maybe it's no coincidence that I got my first inhaler around the same time I started having anxiety attacks. Nick has asthma, so I guess the doctor thought it wasn't a stretch that I'd have it too. Nick's is way worse than mine, though. Actually, I don't know if I've ever had an asthma attack before since I have no way of knowing what's my anxiety and what's my asthma . . . or if I really even have asthma at all. When I was first prescribed an albuterol inhaler, I used it every day, but then I noticed that even when I forgot, I still breathed the same way as usual. Now, whenever I get inhalers, they somehow end up in Nick's medicine cabinet.

When me and my brothers moved to LA, I realized that driving became a lot like breathing. The more I focused on it—specifically, the more I focused on everything that could go wrong while behind the wheel of a car—the more I panicked. Concentrating on it too much, I could even think myself into a full anxiety attack. The car could get T-boned, or a tire could pop and I'd be stranded on the side of the interstate until AAA came, or worse, I could get stuck in a ditch somewhere. Maybe the worst mental battle involved drive-thrus—something I still can't think about too hard.

I don't know why we, as a society, designed drive-thrus like that. Why is it that, at almost every drive-thru, there's the possibility of getting stuck? Say you're in a long line of cars, eight in front of you and eight behind you. If one person's car breaks down or if they just decide they don't want to drive forward anymore, there'd be no way to get out of the line. Most drive-thrus have that concrete curb you'd have to drive over, or you'd have to mow down those orange cones they put up at In-N-Out and risk running over an employee. Unless all eight people behind you decided to reverse, one by one, you'd have to find some other way out and risk messing up your car or causing an accident. The thought of that horrified me.

Back in Boston, I didn't feel as anxious driving or in drive-thrus. Sure, it's a city with lots of traffic, but I grew up there, and without GPS, I could navigate to where I needed to go and make it home from just about anywhere. But LA has different, unimaginable traffic, high-speed chases, and so many more cars and people. I developed a fear of judgment from other drivers on the road or friends in my car when I had to do things like parallel park. My car in Boston was my escape and safe haven, but in LA, there were more anxious thoughts I had to try and overcome.

Plus, when I went out to get fast food in Boston, my family was usually with me, and Nick prides himself on being the best food orderer ever. He's the type to sit down at a restaurant with 12 people and tell the waiter what every single person wants: "He's having this. She's having that." The minivan would be packed with people—my parents, friends, whoever—and Nick would sit in the passenger seat, lean over, and yell everybody's orders into the intercom. Even if he continually messed up Chris's order, which caused hell to break loose as they screamed at each other, at least I didn't have to order for myself. My brothers being in LA with me helped a lot with the drive-thru anxiety, just like with all my anxious thoughts. When I was alone, all I had to focus on was the possibility of getting stuck, but with them yelling at each other about Nick forgetting Chris's fries or asking for the wrong number of nuggets, I could make it to the end, no sweat.

Our manager also helped me with my driving anxiety in so many different ways. As I've said, people don't typically understand the family-like relationship we have with her and her family, but to be honest, they don't have to understand it. When I first came to LA, she and her family gave me so much comfort. For me, when meeting new people, you can tell right away that I'm a shy and anxious person, and she caught on very quickly.

Outside of work, we did so much together, especially with us being good friends with her daughter. Our manager accommodated my anxiety by volunteering to drive us everywhere. Understanding my fear of not having an escape route, she also waited outside in parking lots for us to finish whatever it was we were doing. She encouraged me to drive my brothers and our friends on late-night fast food or 7-Eleven runs when there were fewer cars on the road, so I could gain some comfort and start working toward being able to drive in California.

Since I still struggled with driving, friends picked me up a lot until, after about a year of living in LA, I randomly overcame my worst anxious thoughts. One afternoon, a friend swung by since he and Chris had made plans for everyone to go out and eat at a BBQ restaurant. Nathan was in town for the week; plus, another friend joined us, so that made six people in total. The only problem was that our friend's car fit five. My car fit seven.

Our friend, fully understanding my fear, offered to drive my car for me. I put all of my anxiety to the side and said no. It might not sound like a big deal, but this was my moment to prove to myself that I was capable. At this point, I had been coming to LA for over a year and a half. I knew I had to drive eventually. So, I told them

I would do it. My friend then offered again, but I declined. He said okay and reassured me that, if at any moment I needed to pull over, he would switch with me.

I ended up flawlessly driving the 18 minutes to the BBQ restaurant.

As funny and simple as this situation was, it proved to me how strong our minds are. For *a year and a half*, I made friends pick me up, or I rode everywhere with my manager or in an Uber. Then, one 18-minute drive completely changed my perspective.

Now, whenever I drive, it's as easy as breathing.

What's the Point of Writing a Book?

If you are currently reading this book, the odds are decently high that you've watched one of my YouTube videos. For those of you who have seen me on the internet, I'm so glad you gave me the opportunity to present myself as a writer. And for those of you who picked up this book having no idea who I was, I hope I have made my story interesting and enjoyable so far.

Social media is a rollercoaster that I buckle myself into every day. Connecting to people from all around the world truly blows my mind. By the time this book is published, I will have gone on three national comedy tours with my brothers. During these live shows, filled with real people who I can see out in the audience and take pictures with at meet and greets . . . everything clicks into place and just feels *real*. Comments on social media can only tell me so much about what people think, so in person, when I see excited laughing faces, any negative words I've read online vanish from my mind. Many fans approach me, saying how my content has helped them with their mental battles. That never gets less crazy to hear, especially because I have a problem recognizing what I have done so far. From my perspective, I'm just getting started. I have so many dreams and goals, most of which center around increasing mental health awareness, so it's hard to understand just how much of an impact I've already made. Even saying I've made an impact at all feels a bit arrogant.

I return to one story from our second tour when I think about this. A girl walked up to me before the show. She didn't say anything other than, "Thank you," before placing two pieces of paper in my hands.

"What's your name?" I asked.

"June," she responded.

"It's very nice to meet you." I smiled, placing the papers in my back pocket.

The girl, June, walked away, and the next person in line took her spot in front of me. After speaking to a few more viewers, me, Nick, and Chris went inside to do the show and met even more amazing people. By the time I got back to the tour bus that night, I was exhausted, my voice was halfway gone from talking and shouting for so long, but I felt that indescribable pride that comes after a good performance where everything went right. Ready to crash for the night, I went to change into my pajamas, but then felt something in my back pocket. *Oh, right, the papers from June.*

Sitting in the back of the bus, I read what she'd written.

"Matthew Sturniolo is a content creator who is mostly known for his YouTube videos with his triplet brothers. Although the main purpose of these videos is to entertain, the three of them will often sit down and 'check in' with their fans, as portrayed in videos like 'Q&A + small talk (we love you)' and 'Would you rather + Getting Serious.' However, once Matt expressed his struggles with his anxiety back in May, it resonated with me."

In absolute and utter shock, I flipped to the second page.

"Matt spreads awareness on social media by commenting under the posts of people who struggle with the same mental battles, giving them words of encouragement and positivity. The opportunity was presented to me to see Matt and his brothers in person. Once the flash of the camera went off, I instinctively thanked them for inspiring me to chase my dreams. Anxiety often holds me back from things I want to pursue in the future. This is because of the rush of overthinking and overwhelmingness. However, they've taught me that the most important person who can believe in you is you. Therefore, seeing their faces light up and Matt cheering me on, fist-pumping the air, made me extremely proud of myself and overjoyed with happiness."

By this point, I was on the bus floor, trying to keep it together as I had 11 busmates in the other room.

"Many would challenge the assertion that our past doesn't define us, but humans change every day from the events of yesterday. The actions of one are something that make up who they are as a whole, and it's hard to let go and forget about the past. Our minds are very powerful, and how we react to obstacles influences the outcome. If we forget about the past, then we lose a sense of who we are and what we stand for. Our background is what shapes us."

I folded the two papers and put them in my suitcase to bring home. Sometimes, when I read a hurtful comment online, I pull out June's English essay, now stored in a memory box in my room. It's a reminder of what I have done for some people and that, even if I can only make a positive difference in one person's life, my work matters.

When I first started this book, I thought I was writing it for myself—to get this big weight off of my shoulders and establish myself as a writer. But in reality, I wrote it for people like June, who, in a brief moment of meeting, connected with me more than she thought. She didn't understand the impact of those two pieces of paper she put in my hands. I recognize that chasing my dream of being a writer will be difficult, especially since I've already been placed in the box of "comedy YouTuber," but remembering fans like June, I know that I do not have to fit a certain label to connect with others. That is enough for me to feel complete.

I'm honored to be even a small part of so many people's lives and to be part of such an incredible and supportive community. I am more grateful than I have the ability to describe.

That said, I also know that many viewers picked up this book for an inside look into my brothers' and my lives. Since no one's life is perfect, I'm sure many want to hear what headaches we deal with behind the scenes and the frustrations that come with living in the public eye. But even recognizing this, I still hesitated.

I went to Nick to have a conversation we've had countless times before.

"How much can you complain in the space we're in?" I asked. "How can you share annoyances without sounding like a tone-deaf jerk?"

Usually, he'd talk me or Chris out of saying anything that's "too much," but his answer surprised me. "This is the one time, if any, to say what's on your mind. Be honest."

That made a lot of sense. What was the point of writing a book if I left a major part of the story unsaid? If I didn't tell it now, when would I? My audience deserved the whole truth.

So, here goes.

One winter, my grandmother snatched the hat off my head and looked at me in panic. My uncle had bought us Lids gift cards and blank hats for Christmas. Me, Nick, and Chris, being really into customization, couldn't wait to get our names embroidered on the sides, but my grandmother couldn't believe what we'd done.

"What if someone came up to you in public and said, 'Hey, Matt, come here'? That would be the easiest way to gain your trust so they could kidnap you! They'd know your name!"

I think about this moment sometimes and wonder how my grandma would react if she saw our lives now, fully on display for anyone on the internet to see. What would she say if she knew that fans have shown up at our front door or that we've been followed home from public places?

When we first started out and had no idea how big we'd get, me, Nick, and Chris weren't careful about what appeared in the background of videos: strip mall signs, neon business logos, and street names. It wasn't hard for people to look on Google Maps and find "our McDonald's," where we parked and filmed. Eventually, the McDonald's became so well-known that fans started waiting for us there or honking at us while we filmed. We even developed a weird relationship with one of the workers, who'd let us know that fans were out looking for us when we ordered.

Many times, I've driven back from filming and noticed a car taking the same turns as I am and following at a close distance. Usually, the driver has their phone out or within arm's reach. In those cases, all you know is that you have to lose them before going home and revealing where you live, so you just hope they run out of gas first. My worst nightmare is that I crash my car trying to escape someone who recognizes me—either because I'm going too fast to outrun them or because they cause an accident trying to stay close—and someone ends up getting hurt, whether that's me, my brothers, the other driver, or some innocent bystander going about their day.

What's crazy is that most of the time, these people don't think following us is weird. If they were doing this to any average person, they would have the cops called on them. Imagine going to a random McDonald's, picking a random car in the parking lot, and following it home. That's criminal behavior. It would look like you're plotting a murder. But for some reason, when they try to stalk us around, it's different in their minds.

Our fanbase is one of the biggest blessings I've had in my life, and I wouldn't change it for anything. But within that following, there is the bad side of the internet—the people who have nothing better to do than create false narratives or log on to social media every day, just to call strangers ugly and try to boost their own self-esteem. Yes, the internet is my job, and I've put myself in the position to deal with these challenges, but over time, I slowly started to see more and more of the downsides.

With me struggling to create friendships, I relied on Nick to do that for me, and since most of Nick's friends were women, that meant most of *my* friends were women too. Posting on social media with them would cause an uproar of "shipping" comments and different rumors. I expected this, so it was fine because at least I knew the truth: We were all just platonic friends. I only became upset once I saw comments belittling and bullying any woman for simply being in the same picture as me. This brings a lot of guilt. Even though I'm not the one writing and posting degrading words, I *am* the reason my friends are in the line of fire at all.

Hate comments may be inevitable in this line of work, but I can't lie and say they don't affect me. At the end of the day, I am human. The hateful criticisms of my friends hurt me just as much, if not more, than when people point out my own flaws. Which, trust me, they do plenty of that too.

The internet loves to point out traits I have never noticed about myself. Everything about my private life is put into the world for open discussion. Being shipped with women I've never met, being told that my new haircut sucks, people tracking if I've gained weight, fans trying to figure out why I'm not friends with whoever, and accounts sending my high school ex-girlfriend death threats—and then being told that that's all allowed because I have a good job that pays good money. So much was assumed about my life that I couldn't even wrap my head around it. No matter who anyone is or what they do for a living, nobody should have to deal with this or hear this about themselves.

What's ironic is that, most of the time, content creators do what they do because they don't like interacting with other people. Filming and editing videos is often a solo task that creators do for their own enjoyment at first, but later, realize others like what they're making too. At least, that's how it went for us.

I love to tour and meet all the viewers who allow us to keep doing what we love. Actually, it never hit me how many people watched our videos until we had our first live shows, and I walked into theaters full of people excited to see us. Because me, Nick, and Chris perform as ourselves, not made-up characters or personas, I only feel a little nervous on stage, but without lines to memorize or any way to screw something up, the experience is mind-blowingly positive. Definitely not what I or anyone else expected me to feel, but I'm grateful nonetheless.

The problem is when I'm invited to other people's events. It freaks me out not to have control or know what's going to happen next. Me, Nick, and Chris tend to hate parties, especially LA parties that often involve drugs, alcohol, and a self-absorbed culture. At first, LA confused me, and for a long time, I didn't have the social awareness to know who genuinely cared about my well-being. But with time, I have been fortunate enough to find friends who see beyond followers, likes, and engagement.

My friend, Waylon, for example, told me one of the wildest and kindest things anyone's ever said to me. As a model, Waylon does social media for his job but otherwise doesn't spend a ton of time on the internet. Me, Nick, and Chris were walking around with him one night when he stopped and, out of nowhere, said to us, "I want to let you guys know, just to make sure we have this understanding: If you deleted all your socials tomorrow, I'd still want to be your friend."

I say this a lot, but in LA, I feel like everyone is either the craziest person you've ever met or the nicest. There's no middle ground; no one's normal. Everyone who moved there did so because they wanted to make something of themselves, and they're either cool about that or they're not.

I'm simply lucky to know the coolest people.

Yesterday's Problem

August 21, 2005

Hello boys,

Daddy and Justin are hitting golf balls. We are quietly sitting in the van, probably with about two hours for ourselves. You guys are exhausted. A very fun day at the beach, being pulled around in the big raft, catching fishies (or having Justin catch them), playing in the sand, and running with your nets trying to catch something. Walking back home, being pulled in the wagon. Showers in the outside shower to wash off all the sand.

Life is good! You are two years old, and we have enjoyed each moment of life so far.

I recently read a chapter from a book called *My Monastery Is a Minivan*. Denise Roy writes about a chair in her living room affectionately named "Happy." I think we have chairs like that. Probably the couches in our front room where we sit, cuddle, hug, and get cozy wrapped in blankies. We almost sit on top of each other and, at times, cannot get close enough. We share so many happy, quiet moments together as a family.

"When I sit in 'Happy' and become centered, my children are drawn into this place as well."

I hope that I take you all, many times, to a happy place.

Love,
Mama

When the Sturniolo Triplets YouTube channel hit the highest numbers we'd ever seen, I had the realization that I, Matt Sturniolo, suddenly had a platform, and I had to use that platform for good. There was no question in my mind that, whatever I ended up doing as a career, I wanted to help people like myself. As a kid, I had dreamed of being a YouTuber, but I didn't see any influencers talking about mental health at the time. No one had the same problems, or if they did, they didn't openly talk about them. In the back of my mind, I thought growing a following on YouTube would be impossible because of my anxiety. When I gained that following anyway—not *despite* my anxiety, but in many ways, *because* I spoke out about it—I wanted to be an example for others, the example that I never had growing up. I wanted to be a resource, someone who people could look up to and say, "He's going through something similar to me. I guess I'm not alone like I thought."

The only question was *how* to do that.

Before starting this book, I thought about writing songs for other artists, seeing as I've always had a deep connection to music. Listening to other people's songs has been a way for me to hear my emotions out loud and put them into words that I can never seem to come up with on my own. But that idea went away for a couple of reasons, one of them being that I couldn't sing if my life depended on it. And the other reason is that I couldn't cram my whole mental health journey into a couple of lyrics and make them sound good. I came to terms with the fact that I appreciate music, but I'll happily listen from the sidelines.

I started my own YouTube channel a few years ago, specifically to talk more about my anxiety and mental health, but I quickly realized that those videos weren't the answer either. I can't put nearly enough emotion into that quick 20 minutes—not like I can while I'm sitting down, concentrating, and picking apart my feelings while writing. The other big problem was having to look at a camera while talking about my not-so-proudest moments. I either became so focused on not looking at myself on the camera screen, or I would look at myself for too long, become hyperaware that people would actually watch the video one day, and fumble my words. Wanting to be as authentic and genuine as possible, I never wanted to write a script, but that just meant I'd lose track of what I was talking about and forget my point. And then there was this idea that YouTube videos had to be funny. The urge to make light of my problems and pass them off as a big joke didn't sit right with me. Trying to go from a comedy-based creator to a mental health advocate just wasn't working.

After a while, I realized how much of a passion I have for writing. I guess it's not surprising, considering I grew up around writing my whole life.

On one of my trips back home to Boston, I sat with my mom as she organized her different journals. She stopped to read an entry she had written about 17 years prior. Me, Nick, and Chris ran around our Cape house, giving each other chest bumps, and she hoped we would tire ourselves out and take a nap soon. She continued flipping through the pages and reading me different stories, and with each one, I felt amazed that she could so clearly recall a moment from decades ago.

The week I landed back in LA, I bought a journal for myself and started writing. My mom had inspired me to journal before. Actually, in my childhood bedroom, you could find about 20 different journals with crazy nicknames written on the front of them. A couple of the journals had about 10 entries, while others had about 30. Some with a few words, and some empty. It felt like an instinct, almost as if when something bad happened to me or I got really upset, the voice in my head would tell me, "Just wait until the journal hears about this."

Starting YouTube, I stopped jotting down my thoughts, since I considered our videos a digital journal in a way. But after hearing my mom tell me all those stories, I wanted to try writing again. At first, I mostly wrote down fun stories, like going bowling with friends or where I ate that day, but then I slowly started to work through some of my mental challenges too. Even though my driving anxiety had gotten better, I still struggled with parking, drive-thrus, and driving without my brothers in the car. And during LA events, I still hid in bathrooms like I did in high school to get away from crowds and recollect myself. Journaling helped me look back to figure out why I was feeling certain emotions in certain situations. Yeah, I documented a huge part of my life on YouTube, but that was for everyone online. Journaling was for me.

I was carrying over my anxious traits to LA, not getting rid of them like I thought. My whole life, my parents were by my side, helping me with everything, but I was now across the country, away from them. Yet, the lessons they taught me stay with me wherever I go. I know a lot of my feelings of anxiety and stress stem from when I was a little kid, so when writing about myself in the current day, I catch myself going back to the past. The only times I felt confident were when my mom rubbed my back and said, "Tomorrow is a new day." Even now, I often find myself repeating my mother's words back to myself, except I expand on them more.

"Tomorrow is a new day. Don't let your problems and anxious thoughts of yesterday control your tomorrow," I once wrote in my journal. My mom taught me to take every day one step at a time. I've since expanded on her wisdom and simplified all my worries and anxieties as "yesterday's problem." Yesterday's problems don't need to affect me today.

My journaling sessions started to feel more and more impactful. Writing down simple thoughts allowed me to explore old ideas I hadn't thought about in years and see new perspectives that I'd never considered. For the majority of my life, I let one experience at a baseball game ruin my happiness, over and over again. A big regret is letting my negative thoughts control what would have been happy moments for me. I missed out on nights going to arcades, seeing movies, going to birthday parties, and so much more, just because of the *possibility* of an anxiety attack.

I finally came to terms with the fact that anxiety is an emotion just like happiness and sadness. It would be idiotic to say, "I will find the perfect way to live my life without ever having to feel anxiety again." Just like happiness comes and goes, and some nights I may be more sad than others, the anxious thoughts will rear their heads from time to time. I can't get rid of them, so I need to find a way to live with them. But they won't take away from the days I have ahead.

I began to look at past therapy sessions with a more open mind—now as a 21-year-old and not a child—and try to understand what it was that Jessie and Shelly wanted to teach me. In that first therapy session with Jessie, she had me identify an *Inside Out* character with every one of my emotions. Now I realize why: She was prompting me to connect my feelings with certain situations so that I could identify what made them so scary.

Ten years later, I finally started to use the tools my therapist had tried to teach me. As a kid, I compared my emotions to the characters in *Inside Out*. As an adult, I created my own characters. Paranoia is yellow. Anxiety is red. And depression is blue.

It may seem silly or childish that an adult man uses made-up cartoon characters to express his emotions, but I created these images to help shift my mindset when I feel anxious or overwhelmed. And it works. When I didn't characterize these emotions, I had no way of knowing what I was feeling. Rather than think that the emotion would pass, I thought there was something fundamentally wrong with me as a person, that I would feel anxious, depressed, or paranoid for the rest of my life. But with the characters, I can separate myself from the emotions. They are a *part* of me, not *me* as a person.

Following that train of thought, not including any positive emotions in the list, like excited or relaxed, is an intentional choice. I characterize emotions to separate myself from them, and why would I want to be separated from feelings like joy or thankfulness? When I feel depressed, anxious, or paranoid, my characters help me see that's not who I am. Those feelings have their own identities, apart from my own. But happiness? Humor? Optimism? That's *my* identity. That's who *I* am.

I have been using my characterized emotions for a year now, journaling in different colors depending on my mood. Thinking of my past therapy sessions and past traumas, I, for the first time in my life, feel at peace with my emotions. That's why I started to write this book, and in the time it's taken to write it, I have grown so much more already. But to say I have finally figured out everything would be a lie.

Some things change, and some things stay the same. What I thought I'd be doing after high school is completely different. I am not a therapist, and I am not a firefighter. Yes, I could build a nice birdhouse, but I am also not a carpenter. I am a YouTuber, and when this releases, I will be an author. The career path changed, but the goal didn't.

I may not be a psychologist, but I want to help people understand their emotions, with the message that what they are feeling is normal and valid. The difference is that, instead of talking to a patient one-on-one, I talk to millions of people at the same time through YouTube videos and, now, this book.

When I was 10 years old, I was comfortable with the fact that I would never leave my house again. A lot has happened for me to go from that mindset to where I am now. I've lost friends. I've cried. I've been to therapy. I've moved across the country. I've changed as a person and grown up. And, yes, it was scary and uncertain, but going through all that bad to eventually find the good has been the most beautiful and enlightening journey of my life.

This may be simple and obvious, but I am human. I cannot stress that enough. The internet and social media may confuse things and make people seem more elevated than they are, but the truth is that you and I are the same. If we shut off our phones and log off the internet, we are both human beings. I am not some YouTuber who lives the best life ever, free from struggles. I feel every emotion you feel, and I am not immune to the hard parts of life just because you don't see them on the internet.

No one is greater than the other. We are all equal and play our part on the same planet. I say this because I don't want people to see me as a superhuman or, after reading some stories in this book, an unstable mess. I go to the grocery store. I eat three meals a day. I brush my teeth in the morning and at night—though to be honest, sometimes I miss a night and brush extra hard in the morning. If you ever see me in public, don't think, "Oh, it's the guy who thinks he's so cool because he has a lot of followers." Behind all the pictures and the numbers and the screens, I would love to meet you and have a conversation.

Just because I didn't vlog it when I got dragged out of the car and carried into school in seventh grade doesn't mean it didn't happen or that it's not an important event. With all of the videos I put out into the world and all the pages I write, you will still only know a fraction of my life. I hope, one day, I will hear about a fraction of yours. Even then, we will never fully know everything about each other—and that's okay. I live with my triplet brothers and have been with them almost every day for the last 21 years, and I will still never understand everything they think or do. But at the very least, we can share what is important to us and hope that it connects us to others.

I choose to share a part of myself on YouTube and social media, but that doesn't define my entire experience. I have so many goals outside of content creation that I can't wait to start. I have dreams of writing more books and of turning my ideas of "yesterday's problem" into a community of people like me, who look at mental health as an important and prioritized part of our lives. A lot of what I want to accomplish is for the 10-year-old version of myself, who wanted to see what I see and meet the people I meet, but had a mental block that never let him try.

I want to keep pushing myself to explore the world, even if that only means going to a park and spending more time outside. I have dreams as big as traveling across the globe and as small as going to a party. I am constantly trying to push myself out of my comfort zone for 10-year-old Matt—like writing this book for people just like him.

I want to prove to my younger self that the sleepless nights, missed opportunities, and stress were worth it. Even though he might have been confused before, we are okay now. I do what I do to honor his sacrifice of time, of fun, of childhood. His dreams that once seemed too big to chase don't seem impossible anymore.

I'm proud of him for not giving in when times got rough and for keeping his eyes on the light at the end of the tunnel, even though some days he didn't see it.

Today, I will make a mistake, and tomorrow, I will learn from it. What happened yesterday, even if painful or difficult, will make me wake up stronger tomorrow.

For the past me—and for what happened yesterday—I am thankful.

Acknowledgments

To my family, my heroes, my everything—thank you.

To my mother, the most selfless person I have ever met, I am lucky to call you my mom. You told me that, while growing up, you dreamed of one day being a mother. But you will always be more than that: a support system, a giver, a best friend, and my biggest cheerleader. Your support never did and never will go unnoticed.

To my father, I have always remembered you as a hard worker and a family man. From working doubles and picking up overtime to being there when I caught Chris's championship-winning pitch in my catcher's mitt, your love for your boys and for your family is strong, and it shows.

To my brother Christopher, growing up next to you has been the most amazing thing in my life. The smiles you put on people's faces just by walking in a room is something I have always admired you for. You have the biggest heart in the world, and anyone who gets to know you would say the same.

To my brother Nicolas, growing up with you has been my biggest gift. The strength that you have is truly amazing, and I will forever be impressed by the laughs you can get out of a group. You have inspired me in many different ways, and being by your side has brought me some of my happiest moments.

To my brother Justin, you faced the world before me and showed me that the path is difficult but not impossible. I will always be grateful for having you as a role model. Thank you for being the big brother I wanted and needed.

To Nathan, my best friend forever, you have shown me what friendship means and how family doesn't mean blood. My brother, you have seen me at my worst, my best, and everything in between and stuck by my side. You mean everything to me.

To Madison B., true friends in LA are so hard to find in this crazy city. I somehow got the pleasure of stumbling across you and your family, who have shown me nothing but support for who I am as an individual. Thank you for letting me talk about my book and the creative process with you. Your friendship is something I will always cherish.

To Eileen and Pat, it may not have seemed like it while I was growing up, but the door you opened to new possibilities, just by showing me hospitality and treating me like one of your own, means so much to me. I will forever be grateful.

To Sam, Mason, and Abel, the visual aspects I had for this book are just as important to me as the words on the pages. It means the world to me that I have a team of talented individuals who go above and beyond to make it all happen, all while believing that no idea is too crazy.

To Jamie and Arjan (saved the best for last), working with you has created some of the most memorable moments of my life. When writing a book, I knew I had a lot to learn—but with editors like you, it was fun and safe to be myself. You encouraged me to stay true to my story and my words, and to be myself and have fun with it. This book wouldn't be the same without you. Thank you for being the best editors to help me with my first-ever book.

About the Author

Matt Sturniolo is a YouTuber, content creator, and social media personality best known as one-third of the Sturnolo Triplets, a community that, as of early 2025, has over 7.39 million YouTube subscribers and 9.1 million TikTok followers. Matt co-hosts the *Cut the Camera* podcast, where he and his brothers give an unfiltered look into their everyday lives. In 2023 and 2025, they took their success on the road with the Let's Trip and Surprise Party tours, selling out venues across the US. He and his brothers have also been featured in several major publications, including *Boston Magazine*, which named them the city's "best YouTube power trio."

In January 2024, his brother Nick launched a lip balm brand named Space Camp Wellness, while Chris introduced a clothing line called Fresh Love. Now, Matt's brand, Yesterday's Problem, aims to promote mental health advocacy and create a supportive community for those who struggle with depression, anxiety, and other challenges, his core message being: "Don't let yesterday's problems control your tomorrow."

www.ingramcontent.com/pod-product-compliance
Lightning Source LLC
LaVergne TN
LVHW022204200926
848481LV00006B/1846